Lectionary Worship Workbook

Series IV, Cycle A

Beverly S. Bailey

CSS Publishing Company, Inc., Lima, Ohio

LECTIONARY WORSHIP WORKBOOK, SERIES IV, CYCLE A

*For my mother and father
who taught me to enjoy worship*

Copyright © 2004 by
CSS Publishing Company, Inc.
Lima, Ohio

The original purchaser may photocopy material in this publication for use as it was intended (i.e. worship material for worship use; educational material for classroom use; dramatic material for staging or production). No additional permission is required from the publisher for such copying by the original purchaser only. Inquiries should be addressed to: Permissions, CSS Publishing Company, Inc., P.O. Box 4503, Lima, Ohio 45802-4503.

Some scripture quotations are from the *New Revised Standard Version of the Bible*, copyright 1989 by the Division of Christian Education of the National Council of the Churches of God in the USA. Used by permission.

Scripture references may be paraphrased from many Bible versions, and are not direct quotes.

Library of Congress Cataloging-in-Publication Data

Bailey, Beverly S.
  Lectionary worship workbook. Series IV. Cycle A / Beverly S. Bailey.
    p. cm.
    ISBN 0-7880-2315-2 (binder: alk. paper) — ISBN 0-7880-2316-0 (perfect bound: alk. paper)
1. Public worship—Handbooks, manuals, etc. 2. Common lectionary (1992)—Handbooks, manuals, etc. 3. Worship programs. I. Title.
BV25.B33 2004
264—dc22
2004009882

For more information about CSS Publishing Company resources, visit our website at www.csspub.com.

ISBN 0-7880-2315-2 (binder)
ISBN 0-7880-2316-0 (paperback)   PRINTED IN U.S.A.

Table Of Contents

How To Use This Book   5

Advent Season
First Sunday Of Advent   7
Second Sunday Of Advent   9
Third Sunday Of Advent   12
Fourth Sunday Of Advent   15

Christmas Season
Christmas Eve/Day   17
First Sunday After Christmas   20

Epiphany Season
The Epiphany Of Our Lord   22
The Baptism Of Our Lord (First Sunday After Epiphany/Ordinary Time 1)   25
Second Sunday After Epiphany, Ordinary Time 2   28
Third Sunday After Epiphany, Ordinary Time 3   30
Fourth Sunday After Epiphany, Ordinary Time 4   32
Fifth Sunday After Epiphany, Ordinary Time 5   36
Sixth Sunday After Epiphany, Ordinary Time 6   39
Seventh Sunday After Epiphany, Ordinary Time 7   42
Eighth Sunday After Epiphany, Ordinary Time 8   46
The Transfiguration Of Our Lord (Last Sunday After Epiphany)   49

Lenten Season
Ash Wednesday   51
First Sunday In Lent   54
Second Sunday In Lent   57
Third Sunday In Lent   60
Fourth Sunday In Lent   64
Fifth Sunday In Lent   68
Palm Sunday/Sunday Of The Passion   70
Maundy Thursday   72
Good Friday   74

Easter Season
The Resurrection Of Our Lord/Easter Day   77
Second Sunday Of Easter   80
Third Sunday Of Easter   83
Fourth Sunday Of Easter   86
Fifth Sunday Of Easter   89
Sixth Sunday Of Easter   91
The Ascension Of Our Lord   94
Seventh Sunday Of Easter   97

Pentecost Season Revised Common / Episcopal	Lutheran (other than ELCA)	Roman Catholic	
The Day Of Pentecost	The Day Of Pentecost	The Day Of Pentecost	99
The Holy Trinity	The Holy Trinity	The Holy Trinity	103
Proper 4	Ordinary Time 9	Pentecost 2	105
Proper 5	Ordinary Time 10	Pentecost 3	107
Proper 6	Ordinary Time 11	Pentecost 4	110
Proper 7	Ordinary Time 12	Pentecost 5	112
Proper 8	Ordinary Time 13	Pentecost 6	116
Proper 9	Ordinary Time 14	Pentecost 7	119
Proper 10	Ordinary Time 15	Pentecost 8	122
Proper 11	Ordinary Time 16	Pentecost 9	126
Proper 12	Ordinary Time 17	Pentecost 10	129
Proper 13	Ordinary Time 18	Pentecost 11	132
Proper 14	Ordinary Time 19	Pentecost 12	135
Proper 15	Ordinary Time 20	Pentecost 13	139
Proper 16	Ordinary Time 21	Pentecost 14	142
Proper 17	Ordinary Time 22	Pentecost 15	145
Proper 18	Ordinary Time 23	Pentecost 16	148
Proper 19	Ordinary Time 24	Pentecost 17	152
Proper 20	Ordinary Time 25	Pentecost 18	155
Proper 21	Ordinary Time 26	Pentecost 19	160
Proper 22	Ordinary Time 27	Pentecost 20	163
Proper 23	Ordinary Time 28	Pentecost 21	167
Proper 24	Ordinary Time 29	Pentecost 22	170
Proper 25	Ordinary Time 30	Pentecost 23	173
All Saints' Sunday	All Saints' Sunday	All Saints' Sunday	176
Proper 26	Ordinary Time 31	Pentecost 24	179
Proper 27	Ordinary Time 32	Pentecost 25	183
Proper 28	Ordinary Time 33	Pentecost 26	187
Christ The King	Christ The King	Christ The King	190
Thanksgiving Day	Thanksgiving Day	Thanksgiving Day	193

U. S. / Canadian Lectionary Comparison   197

How To Use This Book

It has been my privilege to work through a church year with the scripture passages selected through the Revised Common Lectionary, Year A. This book is intended to be a starting place for worship planners and pastors. It is my hope that the hymns and anthems chosen, the prayers and litanies written, and the creative methods of presenting scripture will keep your own creative juices flowing with new methods of making worship relevant for all your parishioners.

The church should not be in the business of competing with other forms of entertainment. Throughout history we have relied on the story of faith found in the Bible, but that doesn't mean we simply keep on doing things the way they have always been done. Much research has been done in the last few decades to discover more about the ways people learn. Harold Gardner has written several books about the different "ways people learn," and they include more than auditory learning. The church is a wonderful place to use all of our senses; as well as learning through relationships with other believers.

Therefore, I firmly believe in using art, music, drama, silence, and aroma — in retelling the wonderful story of God's covenantal relationships, and in the life of Jesus Christ and the earliest Christians.

Since I am a musician both by training and by sheer love of singing, I love hymns. I have tried to choose a variety of hymns using five different hymnals. There are also many hymnal supplements and collections of hymns to be found through denominational publishing houses. This is a wonderful time for finding hymns that connect with people. Many churches are offering "praise bands," jazz services, and other alternatives to the sacred music we associate with church. I firmly believe that we don't want to "throw the baby out with the bath water," and think that we can combine many kinds of music in our services. But it takes time and energy to educate both ourselves and our parishioners. The hymnals that I used and their abbreviations are listed below:

- LBW — *Lutheran Book Of Worship*, Minneapolis, Augsburg, 1978.
- PH — *Presbyterian Hymnal*, Louisville, Westminster/John Knox Press, 1990.
- NCH — *The New Century Hymnal*, Cleveland, The Pilgrim Press, 1995.
- UM — *The United Methodist Hymnal*, Nashville, United Methodist Publishing House, 1989.
- CBH — *Hymnal: A Worship Book*, Elgin, Illinois, Brethren Press, 1992.

I used several catalogs in choosing anthems, but I most often chose music I have used in the past. I also looked at books of praise music, and deliberately incorporated the Choristers Guild Catalog (CGA). Choristers Guild publishes music for all ages of children and youth, as well as simple anthems for small choirs. It is very important to include children in worship, and singing in choirs helps children to love the music of the church. It also gives them an opportunity to be a leader during the worship service.

I have based many of the litanies on scripture, as well as the Call to Worship and the Benediction. It is part of my own tradition as a lifelong Presbyterian, but the more our congregations hear scripture read and interpreted, the less foreign it will seem to them. It is my hope that scripture will come alive through the aspects of this book.

Enjoy, plan, and may the Spirit be with you in your own worshiping experience.

First Sunday Of Advent

Isaiah 2:1-5   Psalm 122
Romans 13:11-14   Matthew 24:36-44

Hymns
Sleepers Wake (PH17, UM720, LBW31)
People Look East (PH12, UM202)
Down By The Riverside
Shalom Chaverim (PH587, UM667)
Behold, A Broken World (UM426)
With Joy I Heard My Friends Exclaim (PH235)
Arise, Your Light Has Come (PH411)
O God Of Love, O God Of Peace (NCH 571, CBH368, PH295)

Anthems
Teach Me Your Ways (Artmann)
Teach Me Your Ways (Duncan)
Teach Me Your Ways (Haas)
Teach Me Your Ways (Kreutz)
Teach Me Your Ways (Miro/Steel)
Teach Me Your Ways (Proulx/Gelineau)
You Must Be Ready, John Horman, Lorenz
You Have Put On Christ, J. William Greene, GIA Publications

Call to Worship
(Voices should be in various places in the congregation and stand to read their statement)
Voice 1: Come; let us walk in the light of God.
Voice 2: I was glad when they said to me, "Let us go to the house of the Lord."
Voice 3: Peace be within your walls, and security within your towers.
Voice 4: Let us lay aside the works of darkness and put on the armor of light.
Voice 5: Keep awake for you don't know which day your Lord is coming.
Pastor: On this first Sunday in Advent, let us heed the words of scripture and join together to worship our God.
Unison: Let us pass the peace of God to one another. (Peace be with you, and also with you.)

Lighting of the Advent Wreath Candle (Peace, Light)
(Choose a family from the congregation)

Voice 1: For everyone, 'neath their vine and fig tree, shall live in peace and unafraid ...

Voice 2: Today we light the first advent candle, the candle of peace. Peace is like the flame of this candle — it flickers. Sometimes it lights the darkness, sometimes it is snuffed out, and we must attempt to light it again. *(Lights candle)*

Voice 3: Peace is more than the absence of war — it is the sense of well-being in all people.

Voice 4: God loves us enough to send us the Prince of Peace.

(Congregation sings Shalom Chaverim*)*

Scripture Reading (Choral Reading based on Psalm 122)
1 Voice: I was glad when they said to me,
All: Let us go to the house of the Lord!
3 Voices: Our feet are standing within your gates, O Jerusalem.
All: Jerusalem was built as a city that is bound firmly together.
1 Voice: To it the tribes go up, the tribes of the Lord, as was decreed for Israel, to give thanks to the name of the Lord.
3 Voices: For there the thrones for judgment were set up, the thrones of the house of David.
1 Voice: Pray for the peace of Jerusalem:
All: May they prosper who love you. Peace be within your walls, and security within your towers.
1 Voice: For the sake of my relatives and friends I will say, "Peace be within you."
All: For the sake of the house of the Lord our God, we will seek your good.

Call to Offering
"For the sake of the house of the Lord our God, I will seek your good." Let us now seek ways of doing God's work in the world as we bring our offerings of time and money.

Prayer of Dedication
The psalmist tells us, "May they prosper who love you, O God." As we dedicate these gifts, we show our love for you and for neighbor. Help us to use these gifts in the building of peace in your world. Amen.

Benediction
Leader: Now is the moment.
People: The moment for us to wake from sleep.
Leader: Now is the moment to lay aside the works of darkness.
People: We will put on the armor of light.
Leader: Now is the moment to leave the comfort of community and go out into the world.
People: We go to tell the good news of Jesus Christ.
Leader: Peace and joy go with you all. Amen.

Second Sunday Of Advent

Isaiah 11:1-10 Psalm 71:1-7, 18-19
Romans 15:4-13 Matthew 3:1-12

Hymns
Lo, How A Rose E'er Blooming (UM216, PH48, CBH211, NCH127)
Jesus Shall Reign (UM 157, CBH319, NCH300)
Hope Of The World (PH360, UM178, NCH46)
O Morning Star How Clear And Bright (NCH158, PH69, UM247)
On Jordan's Bank The Baptist's Cry (PH10, LBW36, CBH183, NCH115)
Creator Of The Stars Of Night (PH4)
O Day Of Peace That Dimly Shines (UM729, PH450)
Isaiah The Prophet Has Written (PH339, NCH108)
All Hail To God's Anointed (UM203, PH205, CBH185)
Comfort, Comfort O My People (CBH176, PH3)
Wild And Lone The Prophet's Voice (PH409)

Anthems
Lo, How A Rose E'er Blooming, Praetorius, G. Schirmer, SATB
The Lion And The Lamb, Natalie Sleeth, CGA, Unison (good for young children)
Advent Song, Richard Clarke, GIA, SATB, congregation, keyboard, flute, handbells
Prepare The Way Of The Lord, Mozart/Hopson, CGA, 2-part mixed, SAB

Call to Worship
Leader: Blessed be the God of Israel, who alone does wondrous things.
People: Blessed be God's glorious name forever — may glory fill the whole earth. We come together in hope as we prepare for the coming of our Savior.
Leader: Welcome one another, therefore; just as Christ welcomes you. (Passing of the Peace.)

Lighting of the Advent Wreath Candle (Hope, Righteousness)
(Choose a family or singles from the congregation. The first candle should be lit before the service)

Voice 1: Hope of the world, God's gift from highest heaven, bringing to hungry souls the bread of life, still let thy spirit unto us be given to heal earth's wounds and end our bitter strife. (Verse 2 of *Hope of the World* by Georgia Harkness, 1954)

Voice 2: On this second Sunday in Advent, we light the candle of hope. When we are lost in the darkness, any flicker of light gives us hope. Perhaps we can find our way out of the darkness. Then we can move through the unknown into a new way of being.

Voice 3: *(Lights the candle)* As we light the candle of hope, our thoughts turn to a dark night in Bethlehem centuries ago when a despairing world waited in hope for the light of the world to be born. May we, like the shepherds and Magi, abound in hope and peace.

(Congregation sings Song Of Hope*)*

Scripture Reading (Creative interpretation of Isaiah 11:1-10, including the Prayer of Confession and Assurance of Pardon)
(Have a stool covered in brown cloth or paper to look like a tree trunk sitting on the chancel — tall enough for a person to crouch behind it. Voice 1 and 2 are crouched behind stool)

Voice 1: *(Stands)* A shoot shall come out from the stump of Jesse,

Voice 2: *(Stands, sticks head out around the first person)* and a branch shall grow out of his roots. *(Stands beside Voice 1)*

Voice 3: *(Enters from off stage and stands behind Voices 1 and 2)* The Spirit of the Lord shall rest on him *(Rests one hand on shoulder of Voice 1)*, the spirit of wisdom and understanding, the spirit of counsel and might *(Rests other hand on shoulder of Voice 2)* the spirit of knowledge and the fear of the Lord. *(Moves between Voices 1 and 2)*

Voice 4: *(Joins other three)* His delight shall be in the fear of the Lord. He shall not judge by what his eyes see, or decide by what his ears hear,

Voice 5: *(Joins)* but with righteousness he shall judge the poor, and decide with equity for the meek of the earth;

Voice 6: *(Joins)* he shall strike the earth with the rod of his mouth, and with the breath of his lips he shall kill the wicked.

Voice 7: *(Joins)* Righteousness shall be the belt around his waist, and faithfulness the belt around his loins.

All: The wolf shall live with the lamb, the leopard shall lie down with the kid, the calf and the lion and the fatling together, and a little child shall lead them.

Voice 1: Please join us now in the unison Prayer of Confession.

(As the Assurance of Pardon is read, the children's choir, in animal costumes, comes forward)

Prayer of Confession
The wolf shall live with the lamb, the leopard lie down with a baby goat, a calf and a lion together? We're sorry, God, but we really have trouble believing that. A little child shall lead us? Even as we prepare for the coming of the Christ child, hatred and warmongering are all around us. We want to believe that your creatures can live peaceably together, but we feel no peace in our own hearts. God, grant us hope for a new world order. Let it start here, today. Give us resolve; give us hope.

(Continue in silence for individual prayer and reflection)

Assurance of Pardon (Pastor)
A shoot will come out from the stump of Jesse and a branch shall grow out of his root. That branch gives us hope. Through Christ our Redeemer we can have hope. Christ became a servant on behalf of the truth of God to confirm the promises given to the Israelites. Live free in the promise of Christ.

(Children now sing The Lion and the Lamb *by Natalie Sleeth)*

Voices 1 through 7: The cow and the bear shall graze, their young shall lie down together; and the lion shall eat straw like the ox. *(Family with a baby and small child now come forward and walk across in front of the group)* The nursing child shall play over the hole of the asp, and the weaned child shall put its hand on the adder's den. *(Children's choir and family leave)* They will not hurt or destroy on all my mountain; for the earth will be as full of the knowledge of the Lord as the waters cover the sea.

(Voices 3 through 7 leave)

Voices 1 and 2: *(Representing the stump and the root, they stand behind the trunk of the tree with hands out)* On that day the root of Jesse shall stand as a signal to the peoples; the nations shall inquire of him, and his dwelling shall be glorious. Amen. *(Exit the chancel area)*

Benediction
Leader: May the God of steadfastness and encouragement grant you to live in harmony with one another, in accordance with Christ Jesus.
People: The root of Jesse shall come: the one who rises to rule — in him we shall hope.
Leader: May the God of hope fill you with all joy and peace in believing, so that you may abound in hope by the power of the Holy Spirit.
People: We go out in hope! Amen.

Third Sunday Of Advent

Isaiah 35:1-10   Psalm 146:5-10 or Luke 1:47-55
James 5:7-10   Matthew 11:2-11

Hymns
Lo, How A Rose E'er Blooming (UM216, PH48, NCH211, NCH127)
Cold December Flies Away (UM233)
I'll Praise My Maker While I've Breath (UM60, PH253, NCH166)
Psalter 146 (UM858, PH254)
My Soul Gives Glory To My God (UM198, PH600, CBH119)
Prepare The Way, O Zion (PH13)
Come, Thou Long Expected Jesus (UM196, PH1, NCH178, CBH122)
O For A Thousand Tongues To Sing (CBH110, PH466, NCH110, CBH42)
Santo, Santo, Santo (CBH400, NCH400, UM65)
The Desert Shall Rejoice (PH18)

Anthems
Selections from the *Messiah: Then Shall The Eyes Of The Blind Be Opened, He Shall Feed His Flock,* G. F. Handel
Wait For The Lord, John Horman
Magnificat, Taize
Thou Shalt Know Him When He Comes, Hal Hopson, Harold Flammer, SATB

Call to Worship
Leader: Happy are those whose help is in the God of Jacob, whose hope is in the Lord their God.
People: We rejoice in God our creator, who is forever faithful.
Leader: Our God gives justice to the oppressed and food to the hungry.
People: We rejoice in a righteous God who opens the eyes of the blind.
Leader: Our God watches over the stranger, the orphan, and the widow.
People: Our God reigns forever.
All: Praise the Lord!

Lighting of the Advent Wreath Candle (Joy)
(Choose a couple who are expecting a baby to light the candle. The first two candles should be lit before the service)

Both Voices: Today — the third Sunday of Advent — we light the candle of Joy.

Man: After the angel Gabriel came to Mary and told her that she would become mother to the "Son of the Most High," Mary was filled with conflicting emotions. She went to visit her cousin Elizabeth, who was also pregnant.

Woman: When she came into the room where Elizabeth was sitting, Elizabeth's baby leaped inside of her and Elizabeth was filled with the Holy Spirit. Mary's first words to her cousin were, "My soul magnifies the Lord and my spirit is filled with joy toward God my savior."

Man: As we prepare our homes and hearts for Christmas, may we be filled with pure joy. Today we light the candle of joy. *(Lights candle)*

(Congregation sings Prepare The Way O Zion*)*

Prayer of Confession
Merciful God, we confess that we are not a patient people. We yell at others in the middle of traffic, we grumble about our fellow workers, we constantly judge others according to our own standards. Help us to be patient, God — like a farmer who waits for rain for his crop. Strengthen us, God, during this Advent season. Help us to learn from Jesus, our model and our example of suffering and patience.

Assurance of Pardon
John the Baptist sent his disciples to ask Jesus, "Are you the one who is to come?" Jesus answered, "Go and tell what you have seen here — the blind can see, the lame walk, the deaf hear, the dead are raised." Through Jesus Christ we are forgiven and filled with joy. Amen.

Scripture Reading (Creative Interpretation of Isaiah 35:1-10)
(A choral speaking choir, alternating the verses with the hymn The Desert Shall Rejoice *could speak this scripture passage. The choral speaking choir could be taught the sign language to "The desert shall rejoice, and blossom as a rose" and use it each time a verse of the hymn is sung. Ask the congregation to join in the signing on the last verse)*

All Voices: The wilderness and the dry land shall be glad; the desert shall rejoice and blossom;

Voice 1: Like the crocus it shall blossom abundantly, and rejoice with joy and singing.

Congregation: The desert shall rejoice and blossom as a rose it shall blossom abundantly and rejoice with praise and singing.

Voice 2: The glory of Lebanon shall be given to it, the majesty of Carmel and Sharon.

All Voices: They shall see the glory of the Lord, the majesty of our God.

Voice 3: Strengthen the weak hands, and make firm the feeble knees.

Voice 4: Say to those who are of a fearful heart, "Be strong, do not fear! Here is your God.

Voice 5: He will come with vengeance, with terrible recompense. He will come and save you."

All Voices: Then the eyes of the blind shall be opened, and the ears of the deaf unstopped.

Congregation: The desert shall rejoice and blossom as a rose for the ears of the deaf shall hear, and the blind their eyes be opened.

Voice 6: Then the lame shall leap like a deer, and the tongue of the speechless sing for joy.

Congregation: The desert shall rejoice and blossom as a rose for the tongue of the mute shall sing and the lame will dance with gladness.

Voice 1: For waters shall break forth in the wilderness, and streams in the desert;

Voice 2: The burning sand shall become a pool, and the thirsty ground springs of water.

Congregation: The desert shall rejoice and blossom as a rose for the ground will become a pool and the dry land springs of water.

Voice 3: The haunt of jackals shall become a swamp, the grass shall become reeds and rushes.

All Voices: A highway shall be there, and it shall be called the Holy Way;

Voice 4: The unclean shall not travel on it,

Voices 5 and 6: but it shall be for God's people; no traveler, not even fools, shall go astray.

Voice 1: No lion shall be there,

Voice 2: Nor shall any ravenous beast come up on it:

Voice 3: They shall not be found there, but the redeemed shall walk there.

Voices 4, 5, and 6: And the ransomed of the Lord shall return.

Congregation: The desert shall rejoice and blossom as a rose as the ransomed return to God and come singing back to Zion.

All Voices: Everlasting joy shall be upon their heads; they shall obtain joy and gladness, and sorrow and sighing shall flee away.

Congregation: The desert shall rejoice and blossom as a rose unto Zion we come with joy, for our God has come to save us.

All Voices: The Word of the Lord.

Congregation: Thanks be to God.

Benediction
Leader: Yahweh has brought down the powerful from their thrones, and lifted up the lowly;
People: He has filled the hungry with good things, and sent the rich away empty.
Leader: He has helped his servant Israel according to the promise he made to our ancestors
People: To Abraham and to his descendants forever.
Leader: God's promises extend to all believers — tell the world of these great promises manifested through the coming of a wee baby on a cold December night. Gloria in Excelsis Deo!

Fourth Sunday Of Advent

Isaiah 7:10-16 Psalm 80:1-7, 17-19
Romans 1:1-7 Matthew 1:18-25

Hymns
O Come, O Come, Emmanuel (UM211, PH9, LBW34, CBH172, NCH116)
The God Of Abraham Praise (UM116, PH488, NCH24)
O Hear Our Cry, O Lord (PH206)
Hail To The Lord's Anointed (UM203)
Blessed Be The God Of Israel (UM209)
Emmanuel, Emmanuel (UM204)
People Look East (PH12, UM202)
Savior Of The Nations, Come (LBW28, CBH178, PH14, UM214)
The Virgin Mary Had A Baby Boy (CBH202)
Come, Thou Long Expected Jesus (PH1, 2,UM196, NCH122)

Anthem
Love Came Down At Christmas, John Rutter, Oxford, SATB
From the *Messiah: Behold A Virgin Shall Conceive*, G. F. Handel
O Come, O Come, Emmanuel, Natalie Sleeth, CGA, Unison/descant, SAB
Advent Lullaby, John Bell, GIA, SATB

Call to Worship
Leader: O God, on this Sunday before Christmas, we are thinking about your amazing love for us.
People: Restore us, O God, let your face shine, that we might be saved. (Psalm 80:3) *(Teach the sign language to younger children, have them teach the congregation, and all use when response is spoken)*
Leader: Behold, a young woman is with child and shall bear a son; and shall name him Immanuel. (Isaiah 7:14b)
People: Restore us, O God, let your face shine, that we might be saved.
Leader: A child born of love — God loving us, Mary loving God, Joseph loving God and Mary.
People: Restore us, O God, let your face shine, that we might be saved.
Leader: Love came down at Christmas to show us the way and to save us from our sins. Let us worship our God.
People: Restore us, O God, let your face shine, that we might be saved.

Lighting of the Advent Wreath Candle (Love)
(Ask two or three single folk from your congregation to light the Advent Candle. Light the first three candles before the service)

Voice 1: We have three lighted candles: they represent peace, hope, and joy.

Voice 2: Today we light the candle of love.

Voice 3: On this fourth Sunday in Advent we remember how much God loves us. God gave us the greatest gift we could ever receive. God gave us his son.

Voice 1: Now the birth of Jesus the Messiah took place in this way. When his mother Mary had been engaged to Joseph, but before they lived together, she was found to be with child from the Holy Spirit.

Voice 2: Love came down at Christmas — love all holy, love divine.

Voice 3: Let us remember this all-encompassing love and share God's love with those whom we meet. Let us love one another as God has loved us. *(Light the fourth candle)*

(Congregation sings Come, Thou Long Expected Jesus*)*

Call to Confession
Joseph was a righteous man, who out of kindness planned to dismiss Mary from his life because she was pregnant. He thought he was doing the right thing, but God had other plans. Let us confess our unwillingness to search for God's plan for our lives.

Prayer of Confession
Loving God and Savior, we think too much. We work so hard to try to figure out what we should do. We research our problems on the computer, we ask experts, we talk to friends, but so often we don't leave room for your Word to seep through. Joseph thought he knew the "right" thing to do. So often we're sure of the right thing, too. Forgive us, O God, for not opening ourselves to your Word for us. Open us to your steadfast love. The love that gave us Jesus Christ is there for all of us. Calm us, God, to truly know the gift that saves us and guides us.

Assurance of Pardon
God comes to all of us with saving grace. During this Christmas season, let us remember the loving gift of Jesus Christ who died for us and rose again for us. Behold! Our sins are forgiven. Amen.

Scripture Readings
Psalm 80:1-7, 17-19
Matthew 1:18-25: *Have three men and/or teenage boys read and act out. The cast would include a Narrator, Joseph, and an Angel.*

Charge and Benediction
To all God's beloved, who are called to be saints, Grace to you and peace from God and the Lord Jesus Christ. Please pass the peace to one another, saying, "Peace be with you," and responding, "And also with you."

Go out into the world in peace, knowing that you are surrounded by God's love. Tell the good news of Jesus Christ to all whom you meet. Sing the carols of Christmas with heightened joy for God is truly with us. And now may peace, joy, hope, and love fill your hearts this day. Amen.

Christmas Eve/Day

Isaiah 9:2-7 **Psalm 96**
Titus 2:11-14 **Luke 2:1-14 (15-20)**

Hymns
O Sing A New Song To The Lord (PH216)
Angels From The Realms Of Glory (UM220, PH22, NCH126)
Born In The Night (PH30, NCH152)
Once In Royal David's City (PH49, UM250, NCH145)
The First Nowell (PH56, UM245, CBH199, NCH139)
On This Day Earth Shall Ring (UM248, PH46, CBH192)
What Child Is This? (UM219, PH53, CBH215, NCH148)
Silent Night (PH60, UM229, CBH193, PH134)
The Friendly Beasts (UM227, NCH138)
That Boy-Child Of Mary (PH55, UM241)
While Shepherds Watched (UM236, PH58, 59, CBH196)
Hark! The Herald Angels Sing (UM280, PH31, CBH201, NCH160)
Go, Tell It On The Mountain (NCH154, UM251, PH29)

Anthems
Love Came Down At Christmas, John Rutter, Oxford, SATB
All My Soul This Night Rejoices, Kenneth Jennings, Augsburg, SATB, flutes (optional children)
God's Love Made Visible, Iola and Dave Brubeck, *Lift Up Your Hearts,* p. 40
Coventry Carol, Cynthia Dobrinski, Agape, 3 to 5-octave handbells
Unto Us A Child Is Born, Ken Kosche, CGA, 2-part

Call to Worship
Leader: The people who walked in darkness have seen a great light!
Choir: *(Singing)* Go tell it on the mountain *(Hold note)*
Left Side: Those who lived in a land of deep darkness on them light has shined.
Choir: *(Singing)* Over the hills and everywhere *(Hold note)*
Right Side: You have multiplied the nation, you have increased its joy.
Choir: *(Singing)* Go tell it on the mountain *(Hold note)*
All: For a child has been born for us, a son given to us — and he is named Wonderful Counselor, Mighty God, Everlasting Father, the Prince of Peace.
Choir: *(Singing)* That Jesus Christ is born. *(Hold note)*
(Go right into opening hymn Go Tell It On The Mountain*)*

Service of Carols and Scripture (using Luke 2:1-20)
The cast of characters includes Three Speakers, Shepherds, Angels, Mary, Joseph, Baby

Speaker 1: *(In Roman toga with wreath on head)* In those days a decree went out from Emperor Augustus that all the world should be registered. This was the first registration and was taken while Quirinius was governor of Syria. All went to their towns to be registered. *(Whole cast walks through the sanctuary and goes to back)*

Speaker 2: *(In typical shepherd costume, comes to front)* Joseph also went from the town of Nazareth in Galilee to Judea, to the city of David called Bethlehem, because he was descended from the house and family of David.

(Congregation Sings O Little Town Of Bethlehem, *verse 1. Mary and Joseph begin walk down the center aisle)*

Speaker 2: He went to be registered with Mary, to whom he was engaged and who was expecting a child. While they were there, the time came for her to deliver her child. And she wrapped him in bands of cloth, and laid him in a manger, because there was no place for them in the inn.

(Congregation sings O Little Town Of Bethlehem, *verses 2-3. Could have a solo on verse 2. Mary and Joseph sit at the manger. Mary puts a baby in the manger)*

Speaker 2: In that region there were shepherds living in the fields, keeping watch over their flocks by night.

(Congregation sings While Shepherds Watched Their Flocks By Night, *verse 2. Shepherds come up side aisle and settle on the stage to left of manger)*

Speaker 2: Then an angel of the Lord stood before them, and the glory of the Lord shone around them, and they were terrified.

Speaker 3: *(Dressed as an angel, comes up and stands behind manger)* But the angel said to them, "Do not be afraid; for see — I am bringing you good news of great joy for all the people: to you is born this day in the city of David, a Savior, who is the Messiah, the Lord. This will be a sign for you: You will find a child wrapped in bands of cloth and lying in a manger."

Speaker 1: And suddenly there was with the angel a multitude of the heavenly host, praising God and saying, "Glory to God in the highest heaven, and on earth peace among those whom he favors!" *(Angels run up aisle saying Luke 2:14; they surround Speaker 3. Shepherds get down their knees)*

(Congregation sings Angels, We Have Heard On High, *all three verses. Angels join on the refrain)*

Speaker 2: When the angels had left them and gone into heaven, the shepherds said to one another, "Let us go now to Bethlehem and see this thing that has taken place, which the Lord has made known to us." So they went with haste and found Mary and Joseph, and the child lying in the manger. *(Shepherds get up and go surround Mary and Joseph. Mary sings verse 1 of* Away In A Manger. *Whole cast sings verse 2)*

Speaker 2: When they saw this, they made known what had been told them about this child; and all who heard it were amazed at what the shepherds told them. *(Shepherds and Angels leave)*

Speaker 3: But Mary treasured all these words and pondered them in her heart. *(Reads from the back of sanctuary)*

Speaker 1: The shepherds returned, glorifying and praising God for all they had heard and seen, as it had been told them.

(Congregation sings Joy To The World. *Rest of Cast leaves down center aisle)*

Prayer for Christmas
It's Christmas, God, and we are filled with joy. We've been waiting and preparing, and the day of Jesus' birth has finally arrived. The tree is decorated, the presents are purchased and wrapped, the family and friends have gathered, and we are really ready to welcome you in our hearts. Help us remember the spirit in which you gave us the greatest gift of all — the gift of your son as a tiny baby — a baby who would redeem your people. You gave the gift of yourself because you love us so much. Help us to share that love to a tired, hungry, and hurting world. It seems to us that you are whispering to us, "Share the joy...." We go from this place impelled to do just that. Go with us, God; and give us the ability to spread the good news about the greatest gift ever given. Amen.

Benediction
Leader:	Let the heavens be glad, and let the earth rejoice. Let the sea roar, and all that fills it.
Left Side:	Let the field exult and everything in it.
Right Side:	Then shall all the trees of the forest sing for joy!
Leader:	For the Savior is here. Jesus is here to judge the earth with righteousness.
All:	And the people with truth. Amen.

Choral Response: The refrain from *Go Tell It On The Mountain*

First Sunday After Christmas

Isaiah 63:7-9   Psalm 148
Hebrews 2:10-18   Matthew 2:13-23

Hymns
O For A Thousand Tongues To Sing (CBH110, NCH42, UM57)
Let The Whole Creation Cry (PH256, CBH50)
All Creatures Of Our God And King (PH455, CBH48, NCH17, UM62)
My Faith Looks Up To Thee (PH383, CBH565, UM452)
If You But Trust In God To Guide You (CBH576, NCH410, UM142)
A La Ru (PH45)
In Bethlehem A New Born Boy (PH35) (Closing Hymn)
In Bethlehem A Babe Was Born (PH34) (Opening Hymn)

Anthems
God So Loved The World, John Horman, CGA, Unison/2-part
Glory To God, Hal Hopson, SATB/keyboard
Psalm 148, Gustav Holst, Galaxy, SATB
Coventry Carol, Oxford Carol Book 1, SATB

Call to Worship
Leader: Praise God! Praise God from the heavens and from the heights.
People: Joy to the world! The Lord is come!
Leader: Praise God! All the angels, all the heavenly host!
People: Angels, we have heard on high — sweetly singing o'er the plain.
Leader: Praise God, sun and moon; praise God all you shining stars.
People: O morning stars together, proclaim the holy birth,
Leader: Praise God, you highest heavens; God's glory is above earth and heaven.
Unison: Go, tell it on the mountain, that Jesus Christ is born!

Prayer of Invocation
Loving God, Christmas has come and the feeling of love lingers on. Help us to savor this feeling as our world begins to get back to normal. Help us remember your glorious and generous gift as we begin rushing around again — trying to maintain our crazy schedules. Give us this time in worship to be renewed and refreshed by your word, and to go once again into the world as your creatures — loving, caring, and joy-filled. Amen.

Scripture Reading
Matthew 2:13-23

Litany for all Children in the World
Leader: A voice was heard in Ramah, wailing and loud lamentation. Rachel weeping for her children; she refused to be consoled.

Voice 1 (A mother in Palestine)**:** As a Palestinian mother, I weep because my child was killed trying to go to school today in spite of the curfew. He was shot seven times.

Response: Jesus, our brother, save all who are put to the test.

Voice 2 (from Afghanistan)**:** My daughter was beaten for daring to learn to read.

Response: Jesus, our brother, save all who are put to the test.

Voice 3 (from Appalachia)**:** My child did not get her inoculations. She died from complications after she got the measles.

Response: Jesus, our brother, save all who are put to the test.

Voice 4 (from Russia)**:** My baby froze to death in her crib because we had no heat.

Response: Jesus, our brother, save all who are put to the test.

Voice 5 (from the inner city in the United States)**:** I worry about my son because of gang-related violence. He is afraid of the police because he believes they are racists.

Response: Jesus, open our eyes and help us save all innocent children from the Herods of today. We know you are able to save us.

Benediction
May our God, according to great mercy, be with you as you go out into the world.
May God's steadfast love surround you and give you courage to fight the evil that you encounter.
May God's presence lift you up and carry you through. Amen.

The Epiphany Of Our Lord

Isaiah 60:1-6   Psalm 72:1-7, 10-14
Ephesians 3:1-12   Matthew 2:1-12

Hymns
Arise, Your Light Is Come (NCH164, PH411)
Jesus Shall Reign (UM176, PH423, NCH300)
Hail To The Lord's Anointed (CBH185, UM203, PH205, NCH104)
God Is Working His Purpose Out (CBH638)
As With Gladness Men Of Old (PH63, CBH218, NCH159)
On This Day Earth Shall Ring (CBH192, UM248, PH46)
We Three Kings (UM254, PH66)
T'was In The Moon Of Wintertime (CBH190, PH61, UM244, NCH151)
Brightest And Best Of The Stars (PH67, LBW84, CBH221, NCH156-157)
What Star Is This? (PH68)
O Morning Star, How Fair And Bright (LBW76, PH69, UM247, NCH158)

Anthems
Epiphany Alleluias, John Weaver, Boosey and Hawkes, SATB
Hail To The Lord's Anointed, Allen Pote, CGA, SAB, SATB
See The Glowing Star, (Puerto Rican), arr. Helen Kemp, CGA
Arise, Shine, For Thy Light Is Come, Kenneth Jennings, Augsburg, SATB

Call to Worship
Leader: Arise, shine, for our light has come.
People: We come bringing gifts in praise of the newborn Prince of Peace.
Leader: But where might we find this wonderful child — so that we might pay homage to him?
People: He is everywhere — in our hearts, minds, souls. He is in the people we meet.
Leader: Let us spread the light of Jesus Christ as we worship together.

Call to Confession
We say, "Jesus is the light of the world," and yet we continue to live in darkness. Let us confess our reluctance to move forward into the light of Christ as we pray together our prayer of Confession.

Prayer of Confession
Merciful and ever-loving God, we profess our love for you — our desire to follow you and to live in the light of your dear son Jesus Christ. Yet we do not do so in our everyday actions. On this Epiphany Sunday we seem unable to bring the gift of ourselves to the stable. We continue to succumb to what the material world offers. We want to love you, but we have trouble showing that love to others — even to those in our own families. Come to us, God; help us to gather our resources and come to you — that our hearts might be radiant and filled with the joy that loving you brings.

Assurance of Forgiveness
God loves us and has shown that love through his son Jesus Christ. Come to God in boldness and confidence, knowing that our sins are forgiven through our constant faith in Christ's abiding love.

Scripture Readings
Isaiah 60:1-6: *Have five people sitting scattered in the congregation. Each one will read one verse from this passage. Have them stand with vigor, one at a time, and read their verses in order. When each has finished his/her verse, each walks to the front of the sanctuary and stands close together in a single line. The person who reads the fifth verse should be seated at the front so he/she does not have far to move after reading. The five readers will recite the sixth verse in unison.*

Ephesians 3:1-12: *This would be very effective if memorized by a single individual and recited. That person would start from the lectern and then slowly move forward into the congregation, looking into the eyes of individuals — as Paul might have done in trying to get his point across. Simply reading the passage in the same style could also be effective.*

Matthew 2:1-12: *Have three individuals dressed as early Astrologers enter from the back of sanctuary and travel around the congregation singing the first three verses of* What Star Is This With Beams So Bright, *and ending at the front of the sanctuary. You will also need a Narrator, King Herod, several Chief Priests/Scribes, and a small Child with his mother Mary. Each astrologer will have a small treasure chest.*

Narrator: In the time of King Herod, after Jesus was born in Bethlehem of Judea, astrologers from the East came to Jerusalem, asking,

Astrologers: *(Ask different people in the congregation and ask the ministers)* Where is the child who has been born king of the Jews? We have observed his star at its rising, and have followed it so that we might honor this special child.

Narrator: When King Herod heard this *(Herod comes forward from standing behind the pulpit),* he was frightened that there might be another king, and all Jerusalem was worried also. So Herod called together the leaders of the synagogue *(come up from side)* and asked them where this king, or messiah, was to be born. The religious leaders told him,

Priests/Scribes: In Bethlehem of Judea, for it tells us in scripture.

One Priest: *(Reading from a scroll)* "And you, Bethlehem, in the land of Judah, are by no means the least among the rulers of Judah; for from you shall come a ruler who is to shepherd my people Israel."

Narrator: *(Herod sends one person to bring the Astrologers to him. They talk together quietly)* Then Herod called for the strangers and learned from them the exact time the star had appeared. Then he sent them to Bethlehem, saying,

Herod: Go, search for this child, and when you have found this king, send me word so that I may also go to honor him.

Narrator: After listening to what Herod had to say, they set out and followed that star until it stopped over the place where the child was staying. *(Mary and Child come forward from behind communion table or altar)* The astrologers were overcome with joy, and went into the house. There they saw the child with Mary his mother. They knelt down to see him and offered him their gifts of gold, frankincense, and myrrh. These were gifts meant for a future king. *(Open the chests so that the Child might look in. Mary takes them from the Astrologers and thanks them. Astrologers take their leave and begin moving through the congregation to the back.)* Having been warned in a dream not to return to King Herod *(Still pacing in place)*, they left for their own country by another road.

(Congregation sings last verse of What Star Is This With Beams So Bright *as Magi leave sanctuary. When hymn is finished, Herod leaves the sanctury)*

Benediction
Leader: Go out into the world searching diligently for the child, and when you have found him, spread the joy of this knowledge to all you meet.
Left Side: We will continue our search.
Right Side: We will find Jesus in our hearts.
All: We will spread the joy.

Choral Response: Refrain from *We Three Kings*

The Baptism Of Our Lord
First Sunday After The Epiphany
Ordinary Time 1

Isaiah 42:1-9   Psalm 29
Acts 10:34-43   Matthew 3:13-17

Hymns
Child Of Blessing, Child Of Promise (PH498, UM611, NCH325, CBH620)
Out Of Deep, Unordered Water (PH494)
God Who Stretched The Spangled Heavens (NCH556, CBH414, UM150, PH268)
May The Lord, Mighty God (CBH435, PH596)
Hail To The Lord's Anointed (CBH185, UM203)
There Is A Balm In Gilead (NCH553, CBH627, UM375, PH294)
O Love, How Deep, How Broad (CBH236, NCH167, UM267, PH83)
When Jesus Came To Jordan (PH72, UM252)
To Jordan Came The Christ Our Lord (LBW78)
O Worship The Lord (CBH124)

Anthems
Christ Und Herr Zun Jordan Kam, J. S. Bach, from Cantata 7
Wade In The Water, Spiritual
God Of The Universe, Christopherson, CGA
It Is A Good Thing To Give Thanks, Donald Busarow, Concordia, SATB/handbells

Call to Worship (based on Psalm 29)
Leader: Give to Yahweh glory and strength; worship Yahweh in holy splendor.
People: The voice of Yahweh is powerful and full of majesty.
Leader: The voice of Yahweh breaks down trees and shakes the wilderness. The voice of Yahweh strips the forest bare.
People: And we all say, "Glory! Give us strength!"
All: May Yahweh bless us all with peace. Amen.

Prayer of Invocation
Gracious and generous God, you have given us so much. You have given us your son Jesus Christ as our redeemer and mediator. On this special day when we remember the baptism of Jesus, help us to remember that he was a man of peace. He peacefully came down to the Jordan River where John was baptizing people into a new way of knowing you. John said, "I can't baptize you!" Jesus replied that this was the way it was to be. You acknowledged who Jesus was that day, and Jesus began his ministry of peacemaking. Help us to feel your presence today as we renew our own baptismal vows; remembering your words, "This is my Son, the Beloved, with whom I am well pleased." Amen.

Scripture Readings

Isaiah 42:1-9: *A wonderful depiction of the chosen as a peacemaker, this scripture could be read by women, standing or sitting together as if they were at a stream. Perhaps the flowers on the altar could be cattails and lilies, and the women could gather around the flowers. The women should talk to each other, just as they would if they had gathered for a conversation.*

Woman 1: Here is my servant, whom I uphold, my chosen *(Lifts hands as if holding up a newborn baby)*, in whom my soul delights; *(Other women gather as if looking at the baby)* I have put my spirit upon him; he will bring forth justice to the nations.

Woman 2: *(Clucking at child)* This one will not cry or lift up his voice, or make it heard in the street;

Woman 3: *(Touching flowers and candles on altar)* A bruised reed he will not break, and a dimly burning wick he will not quench; *(Eyes back on baby)* he will faithfully bring forth justice.

Woman 4: This child will not grow faint or be crushed until he has established justice in the earth *(Spreads hands out in front of her)*, and the coastlands wait for his teaching.

Woman 1: *(Bring hands down and steps forward a step)* Thus says Yahweh, who created the heavens and stretched them out, who spread out the earth and what comes from it, who gives breath to the people upon it and spirit to those who walk in it:

All Women: *(Stepping forward to stand together)* I am the Lord, I have called you in righteousness, I have taken you by the hand and kept you; *(Take hands)* I have given you as a covenant to the people, a light to the nations,

Woman 2: to open the eyes that are blind,

Woman 3: to bring out the prisoners from the dungeon

Woman 4: from the prison those who sit in darkness.

All Women: I am Yahweh, that is my name; my glory I give to no other; nor my praise to idols. *(Drop hands)*

Woman 1: *(Stepping forward slowly down the aisle as she speaks, other women following single file)* See, the former things have come to pass, and new things I now declare; before they spring forth, I tell you of them.

Also read Acts 10:34-43 and Matthew 3:13-17. After the sermon, you might do a service of renewal of baptismal vows. This service can be found in *The Book Of Common Worship,* PCUSA, or other denominational service books.

Benediction
Leader: God shows no partiality. In every nation all who know God and do what is right are God's people.
People: God sent us the message, "Jesus Christ is Lord of all."
Leader: That message spread throughout Judea, beginning in Galilee after the baptism that John announced.
People: Jesus then went about doing good and healing all who were oppressed, for God was with him.
Leader: Go and do the same, filled with the Holy Spirit.
All: Let it be so!

Second Sunday After Epiphany
Ordinary Time 2

Isaiah 49:1-7   **Psalm 40:1-11**
1 Corinthians 1:1-9   **John 1:29-42**

Hymns
Jesus, Priceless Treasure (LBW457, 458, PH365, NCH480, UM532, CBH595)
Jesus Calls Us, O'er The Tumult (LBW494, NCH171-172, UM398)
On Jordan's Bank The Baptist's Cry (PH10, CBH183)
Just As I Am, Without One Plea (PH370, NCH207, UM357, CBH516)
Come Gracious Spirit (CBH303)
Like The Murmur Of The Dove's Song (PH314, NCH270, UM544, CBH29)
Spirit Of God, Descend (NCH290, PH326, UM500, CBH502)
All Praise To You, O Lord (LBW78)

Anthems
I Waited For The Lord, Mendelssohn, G. Schirmer, SATB
From the *Messiah: Behold The Lamb Of God,* G. F. Handel, SATB
Little Lamb/Pequeno Cordes, Patterson, CGA
Like The Murmur Of The Dove's Song, White, CGA, Unison/2-part

Call to Worship
Leader: Grace to you and peace from God and the Lord Jesus Christ.
People: We give thanks to our God always because of the grace given us in Christ Jesus.
Leader: God will strengthen you to the end.
People: God is faithful; God called us into the fellowship of Jesus Christ through this church.
All: Let us worship this faithful God.

Scripture Readings
Psalm 40:1-11: *This psalm is another passage that would work well if people sitting in the congregation just stood in place. It should be people who can speak clearly and can be heard, or they should have a microphone. It would be most effective if each verse was read by a different person, who then would remain standing until the end, when all those standing would read the last verse together.*

John 1:24-42: *This could easily be acted out by older children or teens. Cast would consist of a Narrator, John the Baptist, four to five Followers, including Andrew and Simon Peter, and Jesus. Narrator stands at lectern; John and Followers stand in front of or to the side of the pulpit. Simon Peter is sitting on the front row in the congregation.*

Narrator: The next day John saw Jesus coming toward him and declared:

John: *(To his Followers as Jesus walks toward them)* Here is the Lamb of God who takes away the sin of the world! This is the one about whom I said, "After me comes a man who ranks ahead of me because he was before me." I didn't even know him; but I came baptizing with water for this reason, that he might be revealed to Israel. I saw the Spirit descending from heaven like a dove, and it remained on him. I myself did not know him, but the one who sent me to baptize with water said to me, "He on whom you see the Spirit descend and remain is the one who baptizes with the Holy Spirit." *(Pauses)* And I myself have seen and have testified that this is the Son of God. *(Walks with Followers to other side of stage. Followers leave except for Andrew and one other)*

Narrator: The next day John again was standing with two of his disciples *(Jesus crosses in front and stands on side of sanctuary)*, and as he watched Jesus walk by, he exclaimed,

John: Look, here is the Lamb of God!

Narrator: The two disciples immediately followed Jesus. When Jesus saw them following, he said to them,

Jesus: *(As two disciples approach)* What are you looking for?

Followers: Rabbi, where are you staying?

Jesus: Come and see. *(All walk off)*

Narrator: They came and saw where he was staying, and they remained with him that day. It was about 4 o'clock in the afternoon. One of the two who heard John speak and followed him was Andrew, Simon Peter's brother. *(Andrew comes back and draws up brother Simon who is sitting in the front row of congregation)* He found his brother Simon and said to him,

Andrew: We have found the Messiah! *(Walks over to Jesus who has returned and is standing in front of the pulpit)*

Jesus: You are Simon son of John. You are to be called Cephas, or Peter.

Prayer of Dedication (after the offering)
Gracious God, as we bring our meager gifts to you, help us remember the amazement and joy of John the Baptist as he told his followers about Jesus. Let us remember the glee as Andrew greeted Peter with the news, "We have found the Messiah!" May our gifts be given with such glee and may they be used to help others know the joy of finding the Messiah. Amen.

Benediction
Leader: Wait patiently for God. He will hear our cries.
People: May God put a new song on our lips, and may we sing that song to all who will see and hear.
Leader: May all who hear put their trust also in God.
People: Happy are those who make God their trust, who do no turn to the proud, to those who go astray after idols.
Leader: May God's steadfast love and faithfulness keep you safe forever. Amen.

Third Sunday After Epiphany
Ordinary Time 3

Isaiah 9:1-4   Psalm 27:1, 4-9
1 Corinthians 1:10-18   Matthew 4:12-23

Hymns
Canticle Of Light And Darkness (UM205)
To Us A Child Of Hope Is Born (CBH189)
God Of Our Strength (CBH36)
Beneath The Cross Of Jesus (CBH250, UM297, NCH190, PH92)
In The Cross Of Christ I Glory (CBH566, UM295, NCH193-194, PH84)
Lord, You Have Come To The Lakeshore (CBH229, NCH173, PH377, UM344)
Where Cross The Crowded Ways Of Life (PH408, CBH405, UM42, NCH543)
Jesus Calls Us, O'er The Tumult (UM398, NCH171-172, CBH398)

Anthems
He Comes To Us, Jane Marshall, Carl Fischer, SATB
Creator Of The Stars Of Night, Jeffrey Honore, Augsburg, SATB, handbells
The Lord Is My Light, Michael Bedford, CGA, Unison/2-part
Sing And Rejoice With Heart And Voice, Clemens, CGA, Unison/2-part

Call to Worship
Leader: The people who walked in darkness have seen a great light; those who lived in a land of deep darkness on them light has shined.
Left Side: The Lord is my light and my salvation; whom shall I fear?
Right Side: The Lord is the stronghold of my life; of whom shall I be afraid?
Leader: One thing I asked of the Lord, that I will seek after:
All: To live in the house of the Lord all the days of my life. Amen.

Call to Confession
Paul tells us: "For the message about the cross is foolishness to those who are perishing, but to us who are being saved it is the power of God." Let us confess our sins to the God who saves us.

Prayer of Confession
All-powerful and merciful God, the world is a crazy place, and it is often so hard for us to follow the light of your son, Jesus Christ. We want to, but we are weak. We get caught up in petty quarrels and unnecessary confusions. We are like the early Christians who constantly battled divisions among their ranks. There were so few of them, yet they had trouble coming together. Help us, God, as your church, to stop fighting among ourselves and to remember whose we are. Keep our eyes on the light, and help us to follow Jesus.

Assurance of Forgiveness
Jesus said, "Repent for the kingdom of heaven has come near." Jesus is our sure sign of God's redeeming love for us. All we have to do is ask. Alleluia! We are forgiven. Amen.

Scripture Readings

All four scripture lessons are important to the theme and lend themselves to being read in creative ways. It would be important to read the Isaiah passage and the Matthew passage together, but the Psalm passage and the 1 Corinthians passages could be read dramatically.

Isaiah 9:1-4: *This passage would have great dramatic impact if piano or harp music were played as it is read. Play a piece of music that begins somberly and ends very upbeat.*

Psalm 27:1, 4-9: *This passage can be read by an interpretive choir with four solo voices. The whole choir would read verses 1 and 9 and the other verses would be divided up between the four soloists. The choir might stand in a single file line across the front of the sanctuary with each soloist taking one step forward when it is his/her turn, and the rest of the choir stepping forward when they say the last verse together.*

1 Corinthians 1:10-18: *If you have a male member of the congregation who is an actor or has a dramatic flair, have him become Paul for many of your epistle readings. It can't hurt to have visits from Bible characters during the year, and this reading really lends itself to Paul talking personally to the congregation.*

Matthew 4:12-23: *This scripture passage lends itself well to being acted out by older elementary or middle school children. There would only be two speaking parts: the Narrator and Jesus. All other parts would simply be acted out. The cast would consist of Jesus, Narrator, four disciples, and Zebedee.*

Benediction

Leader: Arise; shine, for your light has come!
People: We go out into the world with the light of Christ in our hearts.
Leader: Break the yoke of the oppressors, and proclaim the good news of the kingdom.
People: We go, renewed and refreshed, knowing that God is with us.

Fourth Sunday After Epiphany
Ordinary Time 4

Micah 6:1-8   **Psalm 15**
1 Corinthians 1:18-31   **Matthew 5:1-12**

Hymns
What Does The Lord Require (UM441, CBH409, PH405)
Worship The Lord In The Beauty (CBH220)
The Old Rugged Cross (PH405, UM504, NCH195)
O For A World (PH386, NCH575)
Blessed Jesus, At Your Word (CBH13, PH454, NCH74, UM596)
Blessed Are The Poor In Spirit (NCH180)
Blessed Are The Persecuted (CBH230)
Who Now Would Follow Christ (CBH535)

Anthems
Blest Are They, Haus, GIA, Mixed Voices
Rise, Shine! You People!, Linker, Augsburg/Fortress, handbells
What Does The Lord Require?, Strathdee, *Lift Up Your Hearts,* 97
Ubi Caritas, Taize

Call to Worship
Leader: Hear what Yahweh says: Rise, plead your case before the mountains, and let the hills hear your voice.
People: With what shall we come before Yahweh, and bow before God on high?
Leader: God has told you what is good; and what does Yahweh require of you?
People: Do justice, love kindness, and walk humbly with our God.
Leader: Let us worship God.

Call to Confession
"With what shall I come before Yahweh, and bow myself before God on high?" Let us come to God with a spirit of repentance, acknowledging our sins before the God of justice. Let us pray.

Prayer of Confession
Gracious God, Paul tells us that God chose what is foolish in the world to shame the wise; and that God chose what is weak in the world to shame the strong. So why is it that we keep striving to be more powerful and more wise in the world? Our lives include the struggle to be "great" in our chosen profession, in our sports activities, even in our knowledge of everyday conversation. We feel the need to boast — about ourselves, our jobs, our children, our busy, busy lives. What we should be boasting about is you, God — about your generosity to us, your presence in our lives, your care for the world. Help us to re-order our priorities, God. We want to be the best we can in service to you and to others. Help us remember Jesus' model of ministry, and to rejoice and be glad to do your work in this world.

Assurance of Forgiveness
God is the source of our life in Jesus Christ, who became for us wisdom from God, and righteousness and sanctification and redemption. Thank God — we are forgiven. Amen.

Scripture Readings
Micah 6:1-8: *Read this passage as a litany, using the last few words as a response by the congregation.*

Verses 1 and 2: Hear what the Lord says: Rise, plead your case before the mountains, and let the hills hear your voice. Hear, you mountains, the controversy of the Lord, and you enduring foundations of the earth; for the Lord has a controversy with his people, and he will contend with Israel.

Response: Do justice, love kindness, and walk humbly with your God.

Verse 3: O my people, what have I done to you? In what have I wearied you? Answer me.

Response: Do justice, love kindness, and walk humbly with your God.

Verse 4: For I brought you up from the land of Egypt, and redeemed you from the house of slavery; and I sent before you Moses, Aaron, and Miriam.

Response: Do justice, love kindness, and walk humbly with your God.

Verses 5 and 6: O my people, remember what King Balak of Moab devised, what Balsaam, son of Beor answered him, and what happened from Shittim to Gilgal, that you may know the saving acts of the Lord. With what shall I come before the Lord, and bow myself before God on high?

Response: Do justice, love kindness, and walk humbly with your God.

Verse 7: Will the Lord be pleased with thousands of rams, with ten thousands of rivers of oil? Shall I give my firstborn for my transgression, the fruit of my body for the sin of my soul?

Response: Do justice, love kindness, and walk humbly with your God.

Verse 8: He has told you, O mortal, what is good: and what does the Lord require of you but to do justice, and to love kindness, and to walk humbly with your God?

Response: Do justice, love kindness, and walk humbly with your God.

1 Corinthians 1:18-31 and Matthew 5:1-12: *Something new! Both of these passages talk about whom God chooses to bless. Try reading them from two lecterns, going back and forth with the verses.*

One Reader: The New Testament lessons today are from Paul's first letter to the church at Corinth, chapter 1, verses 18-31, and from the Gospel of Matthew, chapter 5, verses 1-12. We will read the passages alternatively. Listen for the word of God.

Corinthians: Paul states: For the message about the cross is foolishness to those who are perishing, but to us who are being saved it is the power of God. For it is written, "I will destroy the wisdom of the wise, and the discernment of the discerning I will thwart."

Matthew: When Jesus saw the crowds, he went up the mountain; and after he sat down, his disciples came to him.

Corinthians: Where is the one who is wise? Where is the scribe? Where is the debater of this age? Has not God made foolish the wisdom of the world?

Matthew: Then Jesus began to speak, and taught them, saying, "Blessed are the poor in spirit, for theirs is the kingdom of heaven."

Corinthians: For since, in the wisdom of God, the world did not know God through wisdom, God decided, through the foolishness of our proclamation, to save those who believe.

Matthew: Blessed are the poor in spirit, for theirs is the kingdom of heaven.

Corinthians: For Jews demand signs and Greeks desire wisdom, but we proclaim Christ crucified, a stumbling block to Jews and foolishness to Gentiles.

Matthew: Blessed are those who mourn, for they will be comforted.

Corinthians: But to those who are the called, both Jews and Greeks, Christ the power of God and the wisdom of God.

Matthew: Blessed are the meek, for they will inherit the earth.

Corinthians: For God's foolishness is wiser than human wisdom, and God's weakness is stronger than human strength.

Matthew: Blessed are those who hunger and thirst for righteousness, for they will be filled.

Corinthians: Consider your own call, brothers and sisters; not many of you were wise by human standards, not many were powerful, not many were of noble birth.

Matthew: Blessed are the merciful, for they will receive mercy.

Corinthians: But God chose what is foolish in the world to shame the wise; God chose what is weak in the world to shame the strong.

Matthew: Blessed are the pure in heart, for they will see God.

Corinthians: God chose what is low and despised in the world, things that are not, to reduce to nothing things that are.

Matthew: Blessed are the peacemakers, for they will be called the children of God.

Corinthians: So that no one might boast in the presence of God.

Matthew: Blessed are those who are persecuted for righteousness' sake, for theirs is the kingdom of heaven.

Corinthians: God is the source of your life in Christ Jesus, who became for us wisdom from God, and righteousness and sanctification and redemption.

Matthew: Blessed are you when people revile you and persecute you and utter all kinds of evil against you falsely on my account.

Corinthians: In order that, as it is written, "Let the one who boasts, boast in the Lord."

Matthew: Rejoice and be glad, for your reward is great in heaven, for in the same way they persecuted the prophets who were before you.

Call to Offering
Jesus said, "Blessed are the poor in spirit, blessed are the meek, blessed are those who hunger and thirst for righteousness, blessed are the peacemakers." Let us give a portion of what we earn, and have it work for peace and to end suffering.

Prayer of Dedication
All-loving God, Jesus gives us ways of working toward a peaceable kingdom in this world. May what we have given today all be used as blessings for those who need it. Let us rejoice and be glad for what has been freely given. In Jesus' name, Amen.

Benediction
Leader: All right. We know what to do. Go from this place to serve God and love God forever.
People: We go to do justice and love kindness. And walk humbly with our God.
Leader: The important word is "with" — not "lagging behind" or "hurrying ahead." Have patience.
People: We go, trying to be patient, into an unjust world. We go with gladness, for our reward is great.

Fifth Sunday After Epiphany
Ordinary Time 5

Isaiah 58:1-9a (9b-12)   **Psalm 112:1-9 (10)**
1 Corinthians 2:1-12 (13-16) **Matthew 5:13-20**

Hymns
Hail To The Lord's Anointed (LBW87, CBH185, NCH104, UM203)
When I Survey The Wondrous Cross (PH100, 101, CBH259, 260, NCH224, UM298, 299, LBW482)
Break Forth, O Beauteous Heavenly Light (CBH203, NCH140, PH26, UM223)
God Of Grace And God Of Glory (CBH366, NCH436, PH420, UM577)
You Are Salt For The Earth (CBH226, NCH181)
This Little Light Of Mine (CBH401, NCH524, 525, UM585)
Ask Me What Great Thing I Know (NCH49, UM192, PH433)
There's A Spirit In The Air (NCH294, UM192, PH433)

Anthems
We Praise You For The Sun, Mahnke, CGA, Unison
Every Time I Feel The Spirit, William Dawson, Tuskegee Music Press, SATB or TTBB
Set The Sun Dancing, Helen Kemp, CGA, Unison

Call to Worship (based on Psalm 112)
Leader: Praise Yahweh! Happy are those who fear God, who greatly delight in God's commandments.
People: Their descendants will be mighty in the land; the generation of the upright will be blessed.
Leader: They rise in the darkness as a light for the upright; they are gracious, merciful, and righteous.
People: Those who deal generously and conduct their affairs with justice will be blessed.
Leader: For the righteous will never be moved.
All: They will be remembered forever.

Call to Confession
Day after day we seek God; we call out, but do not listen. Let us confess to God our hesitance to listen to God's words. Let us pray together, first silently, then individually, and then together.

Prayer of Confession
Great and merciful God, the prophet Isaiah tells us that you desire our company; that you want to work with us in loosening the bonds of oppression. But we are too busy with our own lives to see the torment of others. We know that you want us to feed the hungry, help the homeless, and clothe the naked. We know that you want us to pay attention to the plight of those people in countries that know no freedom. We hear your call, but we do not heed it. Forgive us, God. Instill in us the desire to do your work in this world. We love you — help us to show that love to those who need it most. Amen.

Assurance of Forgiveness
Isaiah tells us that if we call upon God, God will answer; when we cry for help, God will say, "Here I am." God, when we cry out, you give us the gift of redemption by giving us the gift of Jesus Christ. Christ lived for us, died for us, and lives again. Hallelujah! We are forgiven.

Scripture Readings
Isaiah 58:1-9a: *This passage lends itself well to a choral speaking choir. If you have enough participants, they can be placed around the outside of the congregation, surrounding them with sound. Ten to twelve voices would be the minimum for this passage.*

All: Shout out; do not hold back!

Voice 1: Lift up your voice like a trumpet! Announce to my people their rebellion, to the house of Jacob their sins.

Voice 2: Yet day after day they seek me.

Voice 3: And delight to know my ways,

Voices 2 and 3: As if they were a nation that practiced righteousness and did not forsake the ordinance of their God.

Voice 4: They ask of me righteous judgments;

Voices 1-4: They delight to draw near to God.

All: Why do we fast, but you do not see? Why do we humble ourselves, but you do not notice?

Voice 5: Look, you serve your own interest on your fast day, and oppress all your workers.

Voice 6: Look, you fast only to quarrel and to fight and to strike with a wicked fist.

Voices 5 and 6: Is such the fast that I choose, a day to humble oneself?

Voices 1-6: Is it to bow down the head like a bulrush, and to lie in sackcloth and ashes?

All: Will you call this a fast, a day acceptable to the Lord?

Voice 7: Is not this the fast that I choose; to loose the bonds of injustice,

Voice 8: To undo the thongs of the yoke,

Voice 9: To let the oppressed go free, and to break every yoke?

Voice 10: Is it not to share your bread with the hungry,

Voice 11: and bring the homeless poor into your house;

Voice 12: when you see the naked, to cover them, and not to hide yourself from your own kin?

Voices 10-12: Then your light shall break forth like the dawn

Voices 7-9: And your healing shall spring up quickly.

Voices 4-6: Your vindicator shall go before you;

Voices 1-3: The glory of the Lord shall be your rear guard.

All: Then you shall call, and the Lord will answer; you shall cry for help, and he will say, "Here I am."

Matthew 5:13-20: *This passage is part of the Sermon on the Mount. It works best if you have a storyteller who can memorize the passage and then retell it as if he is in the midst of a crowd of people, teaching them. Move up and down the center aisle. Establish eye contact with parishioners.*

Call to Offering
What God has prepared for those who love God will be revealed to us by the Holy Spirit. Let us prepare to share God's gifts with others by giving generously in this morning's offering.

Prayer of Dedication
Gracious and loving God, we bring our gifts today because we want to help those who are less fortunate than ourselves. We have been given great gifts through your loving kindness, and we want those around the world to know that love. Accept our offering and use it to further your work, so that we might better understand the gifts you have bestowed on us. Amen.

Benediction
"What no eye has seen, nor ear heard, nor the human heart conceived, what God has prepared for those who love him...." Go today with open heart and open hands to accept all that God offers you. Use all your senses to understand the richness of God's gifts in the world. Use that understanding to help others. And may the peace which passes all understanding fill your hearts and minds with the love of God. Amen.

Sixth Sunday After Epiphany
Ordinary Time 6

Deuteronomy 30:15-20 **Psalm 119:1-8**
1 Corinthians 3:1-9 **Matthew 5:21-37**

Hymns
Lord Jesus, Think On Me (LBW309, PH301, CBH526)
Blest Are The Uncorrupt In Heart (PH223)
The Word Of God Is Solid Ground (CBH314)
What Gift Can We Bring (NCH370, UM8, CBH385)
Now In The Days Of Youth (NCH350)
If I Have Been The Source Of Pain (NCH544)
Where Charity And Love Prevail (NCH396, UM549, CBH305, LBW126)
O Christ, Our Hope (LBW300)

Anthems
The House Of The Lord, Ker, CGA, 2-part
Faith Of Our Fathers, Greg Kerkorian, Blake State, 3-octave handbells
Thy Word Is A Lantern, Robert Powell, Abingdon, SATB

Call to Worship (based on Psalm 119)
Leader: Happy are those whose way is blameless, who walk in the law of God.
People: Happy are those who keep God's decrees, who seek God with their whole heart, who also do no wrong, but walk in God's ways.
Leader: O may our ways be steadfast in keeping your statutes.
People: We will praise you with an upright heart.
All: When we learn your righteous ordinances, we will observe your statutes. Let us worship God.

Call to Confession
Paul tells us that we may plant the seed and others may water, but only God gives the growth. Let us come together asking God to help us grow in obedience to God's word. Let us pray.

Prayer of Confession
Loving God, why do we fight with each other? We are your people, and yet we hurt each other and turn away from those we love. We treat those whom we love so badly. We take sides and refuse to listen to what others might have to say. We get stuck and can't seem to learn from other well-meaning people, even here at church. Help us, God. We know that we come together for a common purpose — to learn your desires for us, and to do your work in this chaotic world. Open our hearts to show kindness to those whom we love, and to those we don't even know. As Paul tell us, "We are God's servants, working together." Forgive us, God, for our inability to work toward a new community of love.

Assurance of Forgiveness
Jesus took his disciples to task because they argued with each other and had trouble seeing the bigger picture. But Jesus showed us the love that he had for all people by giving up his life for our sake. God loves us so much that we are forgiven through grace. Amen.

Scripture Readings
Deuteronomy 30:15-20: *This passage is a soliloquy by Moses as the Israelites get ready to go into the promised land. This segment is full of emotion and should be memorized and given as a speech. A good response from the congregation, after it has been given, might be, "We choose life. Be with us, Yahweh."*

1 Corinthians 3:1-9: *This is another good passage either to be memorized or simply read dramatically. It is Paul, speaking from the heart. The response at the end of the reading might be:*

Reader: Only God gives the growth.

People: We have a common purpose. We are God's servants, working together.

Matthew 5:21-37: *This passage is a continuation of the Sermon on the Mount. It can either be read by two voices, a choral speaking choir in which half the group are on one side of the sanctuary and the other half across from them, or as a responsive reading by reader and congregation.*

Voice 1: You have heard that it was said to those of ancient times, "You shall not murder"; and "whoever murders shall be liable to judgment."

Voice 2: But I say to you that if you are angry with a brother or sister, you will be liable to judgment: and if you insult a brother or sister, you will be liable to the council; and if you say, "You fool," you will be liable to the hell of fire.

Voice 1: So when you are offering your gift at the altar, if you remember that your brother or sister has something against you, leave your gift there before the altar and go;

Voice 2: First be reconciled to your brother or sister, and then come to terms and offer your gift.

Voice 1: Come to terms quickly with your accuser while you are on the way to court with him,

Voice 2: Or your accuser may hand you over to the judge, and the judge to the guard, and you will be thrown into prison.

All: Truly I tell you, you will never get out until you have paid the last penny.

Voice 1: You have heard that it was said, "You shall not commit adultery."

Voice 2: But I say to you that everyone who looks at a woman with lust has already committed adultery with her in his heart.

Voice 1: If your right eye causes you to sin, tear it out and throw it away; it is better for you to lose one of your members than for your whole body to be thrown into hell.

Voice 2: And if your right hand causes you to sin, cut it off and throw it away; it is better for you to lose one of your members than for your whole body to go into hell.

Voice 1: It was also said, "Whoever divorces his wife, let him give her a certificate of divorce."

Voice 2: But I say to you, that anyone who divorces his wife, except on the grounds of unchastity, causes her to commit adultery; and whoever marries a divorced woman commits adultery.

Voice 1: Again, you have heard that it was said to those of ancient times, "You shall not swear falsely, but carry out the vows you have made to the Lord."

Voice 2: But I say to you, do not swear at all, either by heaven, for it is the throne of God, or by the earth, for it is his footstool, or by Jerusalem, for it is the city of the great King.

Voice 1: And do not swear by your head, for you cannot make one hair white or black.

Voice 2: Let your word be "Yes, Yes," or "No, No"; anything more than this comes from the evil one.

Benediction
Leader: Choose life so that you and your descendants may live loving, obeying, and holding fast to God.
People: That is life to God's people.
Leader: Neither the one who plants nor the one who waters is anything,
People: Only God gives the growth.
Leader: The one who plants and the one who waters have a common purpose.
People: We are God's servants, working together. Let us plant God's message in the hearts of others.
Leader: In the name of Christ who showed us the power of reconciling love. Amen.

Seventh Sunday After Epiphany
Ordinary Time 7

Leviticus 19:1-2, 9-18   **Psalm 119:33-40**
1 Corinthians 3:10-11, 16-23   **Matthew 5:38-48**

Hymns
O Love, How Deep, How Broad, How High (LBW88, PH83, NCH209, UM267)
Christ Is Made The Sure Foundation (PH416, 417, NCH400, UM559, LBW367)
The Church's One Foundation (CBH311, NCH386, UM545, 546, PH442, LBW369)
How Firm A Foundation (CBH567, NCH407, UM529, PH361, LBW507)
Teach Me Thy Truth (CBH538)
My Hope Is Built On Nothing Less (NCH403, UM368, PH379, CBH343, LBW293, 294)
How Can I Keep From Singing (NCH476, CBH580)
I Would Be True (NCH492)

Anthems
Dear Lord, Lead Me Day By Day, Marshall, CGA, Unison
Shine, Jesus, Shine, Graham Kendrick, *Lift Up Your Hearts,* p. 50
Walk An Extra Mile, Cool, CGA, Unison

Call to Worship (based on Psalm 119)
Leader: Teach me, O God, the way of your statutes, and I will observe it to the end.
People: Give us understanding, that we may keep your law and observe it with all our hearts.
Leader: Lead us in the path of your commandments, for we delight in it.
People: We have longed for your precepts.
Leader: We come to worship and praise our God.

Call to Confession
Paul says, "If you think that you are wise in this age, you should become fools so that you may become wise. For the wisdom of this world is foolish with God." Let us admit our foolishness and ask for forgiveness from our wise God.

Prayer of Confession
Merciful God, we certainly want people to think that we're special. We want them to think we are wise or clever, just a notch above the "madding crowd." Why do we waste so much energy on what other people think? We know that what is important is what you think. And you already know our shortcomings and our foibles — and you love us, anyway. You know what gifts we have and what we are capable of, and you urge us forward. You don't make fun of us when we're down, or laugh at our awkwardness. You simply guide us in moving forward again. Paul reminds us that we belong to Christ, and that Christ belongs to you. Forgive us, God, and continue to guide us through our own foolishness. Amen.

Assurance of Forgiveness
The church's one foundation is Jesus Christ, her Lord. No one can lay any foundation other than the one God has laid. Christ is our foundation, also, amidst toil and tribulation and tumult; we wait the consummation that only Christ can give. We know that in Christ we are forgiven. Amen.

Scripture Readings
Leviticus 19:1-2 (Add verses 3-4), 9-18: *We don't read Leviticus very often in church, but this is a very good passage to read, having the congregation reply, "I am the Lord your God." It can be done with two readers or a choral speaking choir divided in half.*

Reader 1: The Lord said to Moses, saying:

Reader 2: Speak to all the congregation of the people of Israel and say to them: You shall be holy, for I the Lord your God am holy.

Reader 1: You shall each revere your mother and father, and you shall keep my sabbaths:

Congregation: I am the Lord your God.

Reader 2: Do not turn to idols or make case images for yourselves:

Congregation: I am the Lord your God.

Reader 1: When you reap the harvest of your land, you shall not reap to the very edges of your field, or gather the gleanings of your harvest.

Reader 2: You shall not strip your vineyard bare, or gather the fallen grapes of your vineyard; you shall leave them for the poor and the alien:

Congregation: I am the Lord your God.

Reader 1: You shall not steal; you shall not deal falsely; and you shall not lie to one another.

Reader 2: And you shall not swear falsely by my name, profaning the name of your God:

Congregation: I am the Lord your God.

Reader 1: You shall not defraud your neighbor; you shall not steal; and you shall not keep for yourself the wages of a laborer until morning.

Reader 2: You shall not revile the deaf or put a stumbling block before the blind; you shall fear your God:

Congregation: I am the Lord your God.

Reader 1: You shall not render an unjust judgment; you shall not be partial to the poor or defer to the great: with justice you shall judge your neighbor.

Reader 2: You shall not go around as a slanderer among your people, and you shall not profit by the blood of your neighbor:

Congregation: I am the Lord your God.

Reader 1: You shall not hate in your heart anyone of your kin; you shall reprove your neighbor, or you will incur guilt yourself.

Reader 2: You shall not take vengeance or bear a grudge against any of your people, but you shall love your neighbor as yourself:

Congregation: I am the Lord your God.

Matthew 5:38-48: *Continuing on in Jesus' teaching on the mount, this familiar passage could be done well with a small choral speaking choir of five people. If they are strong readers they may be spread out across the front of the sanctuary; otherwise, a small semicircle in the center would work well.*

Voice 1: You have heard that it was said, "An eye for an eye and a tooth for a tooth."

Voice 2: But I say to you, Do not resist an evildoer.

Voice 3: But if anyone strikes you on the right cheek, turn the other also;

Voice 4: And if anyone wants to sue you and take your coat, give your cloak as well;

Voice 5: And if anyone forces you to go one mile, go also the second mile.

All Voices: *(Take one step forward in unison)* Give to everyone who begs from you, and do not refuse anyone who wants to borrow from you.

Voice 1: You have heard that it was said, "You shall love your neighbor and hate your enemy."

Voice 2: But I say to you, love your enemies and pray for those who persecute you,

Voice 3: So that you may be children of your Father in heaven; for he makes his sun rise on the evil and on the good, and sends rain on the righteous and on the unrighteous.

Voice 4: For if you love those who love you, what reward do you have: Do not even the tax collectors do the same?

Voice 5: And if you greet only your brothers and sisters, what more are you doing than others? Do not even the Gentiles do the same?

All Voices: *(Take one forward in unison)* Be perfect, therefore, as your heavenly Father is perfect.

Call to Offering
Jesus says, "Give to everyone who begs from you. Do not refuse anyone who wants to borrow from you. Love your enemies. Pray for those who persecute you." As we bring our morning offering, let us remember all those we help with our generosity. Let us step out of our comfort zones, and give to more than only brothers and sisters we know. The ushers will now wait upon us.

Prayer of Dedication
Gracious God, Jesus challenges us to perfection. May our gifts this morning take us one step further toward the perfect world for which we all long. May our gifts help those who are hungry, war-torn, homeless, and hopeless. May our gifts go to those who are different than us, and unsure in their world. May we truly begin to make a difference in our world. With Jesus' love. Amen.

Benediction
Leader: How firm a foundation, you saints of God, is laid for your faith in God's excellent word.
People: God tells us not to fear, that we will be strengthened, and can stand tall in God's love.
Leader: Fear not, God is with us, we will not be dismayed.
People: God goes with us through trial and tribulation. We go filled with the promise of God's steadfastness and companionship.
Leader: Go in love, go in joy, go in peace — filled with the confidence that God is here!

Eighth Sunday After Epiphany
Ordinary Time 8

Isaiah 49:8-16a   **Psalm 131**
1 Corinthians 4:1-5   **Matthew 6:24-34**

Hymns
Jesus, Priceless Treasure (LBW457, 458, PH365, CBH595, NCH480, UM532)
As With Gladness Men Of Old (LBW82, PH63, CBH218, NCH159)
In Christ There Is No East Or West (PH439, 440, CBH306, NCH394, 395, UM548, LBW359)
All Things Bright And Beautiful (PH267, CBH156, NCH31, UM147)
Seek Ye First (PH333, CBH324, UM405)
Softly And Tenderly Jesus Is Calling (CBH491, NCH449, UM348)
This Is My Father's World (CBH154, UM144, PH293, LBW554)
Joyful, Joyful, We Adore You (NCH4, UM89, PH464, CBH71, LBW551)

Anthems
Consider The Lilies, Sleeth, CGA, Unison
Consider The Lilies, Sleeth/Marshall, CGA, 2-part mixed
Canticle Of Trust, Richard Purvis, Sacred Music, SATB

Call to Worship (based on Isaiah 49)
Leader: Sing for joy, O heavens, and exult, O earth;
People: Break forth, O mountains, into singing!
Leader: For the Lord has comforted his people and will have compassion on his suffering ones.
People: God has inscribed us on the palms of his hands.
All: God is great and God is good. Let us worship God.

Call to Confession
Jesus tells us not to worry about earthly things, but we never listen. Let us bring those worries to God, and ask for forgiveness for wasting precious energy on being anxious.

Prayer of Confession
Calm and loving God, Jesus tells us not to worry about our lives — what we eat or drink, what we wear or how we look. But, we do that, O God — and so much more. Anxiety fills us. "What will people think if I do this?" or "Oh, I'm such a klutz — no one will ever like me." Forgive us, God, for wasting precious time worrying about the little things. Help us to turn our anxiety over to you — to let you guide our thoughts and actions. Let our worries be turned to little joys as we go about our daily lives. We want to strive first for the kingdom of God and your righteousness, knowing that you give us all we need. Help us to say, "I won't worry about tomorrow. God is here with me today." Amen.

Assurance of Forgiveness
Jesus tells us that our heavenly Father knows what we need. God gave us all we need in the gift of his Son, Jesus, the Christ. And Jesus gave us the greatest gift, that of his life, so that we may always know we are forgiven. By his resurrection we know that we are also redeemed to new life. Alleluia! Amen.

Scripture Readings
Isaiah 49:8-16a: *This passage is wonderfully liturgical and perfect for a choral speaking choir. Arrange the choir in this manner:*

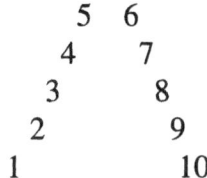

All Voices: Thus says the Lord,

Voice 1: In a time of favor I have answered you;

Voice 10: On a day of salvation I have helped you;

Voice 2: I have kept you and given you as a covenant to the people.

Voice 9: to establish the land,

Voice 3: To apportion the desolate heritages;

Voices 1-5: Saying to the prisoners,

Voices 6-10: Come out,

Voices 1-5: To those who are in darkness,

Voices 6-10: Show yourself.

Voice 8: They shall feed along the ways, on all the bare heights shall be their pasture;

Voice 4: They shall not hunger or thirst, neither scorching wind nor sun shall strike them down,

Voice 7: For he who has pity on them will lead them.

Voice 5: And by springs of water will guide them.

Voice 6: And I will turn all my mountains into a road, and my highways shall be raised up.

Voices 1-3: Lo, these shall come from far away,

Voices 8-10: And lo, these from the north and from the west,

Voices 4-7: And these from the land of Syrene.

All Voices: Sing for joy, O heavens, and exult, O earth; break forth, O mountains, into singing!

Voices 1-5: For the Lord has comforted his people,

Voices 6-10: The Lord has forsaken me;

All Voices: My Lord has forgotten me.

Voice 1: Can a woman forget her nursing child,

Voice 10: Or show no compassion for the child of her womb?

Voices 2-3: Even those may forget

Voices 8-9: Yet I will not forget you.

Voices 4-7: See, I have inscribed you on the palms of my hands;

All Voices: Your walls are continually before me.

Matthew 6:24-34: *This passage is a good one to be memorized and given as if Jesus were talking informally to a large group of people. It is still part of the Sermon on the Mount. It might be well done by a member of your youth group — one who is involved in forensics or debate at their school.*

Prayer after the Offering
God, may the gifts we bring today help to bring solace to those in need. May our gifts serve to alleviate worry for those who have no food, no proper clothes, no clean water. May we provide comfort to others as we seek your kingdoms on earth. Amen.

Benediction
Leader: Go out into this day filled with purpose and joy!
People: We go as birds of the air, knowing that our God will care for us. Our hearts are lightened by that knowledge.
Leader: Seek ye first the kingdom of God and God's righteousness.
People: And all things shall be given unto us. Alleluia!
Leader: May the grace of God, the love of Christ, and the energy of the Holy Spirit fill our hearts with joy! Amen.

The Transfiguration Of Our Lord
Last Sunday After Epiphany

Exodus 24:12-18   **Psalm 2; Psalm 99**
2 Peter 1:16-21   **Matthew 17:1-9**

Hymns
Why Are Nations Raging? (PH459)
O Morning Star, How Fair And Bright (PH69)
Take Time To Be Holy (UM395)
How Brightly Beams (CBH222)
Swiftly Pass The Clouds Of Glory (PH73)
Jesus On The Mountain Peak (CBH232, PH74, UM260)
O Wondrous Sight, O Vision Fair (PH75, UM258, NCH184)
We Have Come At Christ's Own Bidding (NCH182)
Jesus, Take Us To The Mountain (NCH183)

Anthems
Christ Upon The Mountain Peak, Bertalot, Hope, SATB
Precious Lord, Take My Hand, arr. Schrader, Hope, SATB
Jesus, Son Of God Most High, Cox/Lindh, Unison, optional descant, congregation, guitar, flute
Jubilate!, Curtwright, CGA, 2-part

Call to Worship
Leader: Our God is a mighty God! Let all the people tremble.
People: We will praise your great and awesome name. You are holy.
Leader: Mighty God, lover of justice, you have established equity; you have executed justice and righteousness in Jacob.
People: Extol our God, and worship at the holy mountain; for our God is holy.

Prayer of Invocation
Tranforming God, today we come to celebrate the transfiguration of your son, Jesus Christ. That day on the mountain peak our image of Jesus changed, and that story causes our own hearts to change. This story is so hard to believe, just as so much of what you ask of us is hard to accept and believe. Transform us, O God. Help us to know that anything is possible with you. As our world continues to change around us, we often feel powerless to do anything that will be helpful, but we know that we have you on our side, and that we can help change hearts and minds through you. Transform us today, God, as we listen to the stories and hear your word interpreted, as we sing the songs that bring solace to our souls, and as we pray together. All this we ask in the name of Jesus, the Christ. Amen.

Scripture Readings
It would be helpful in hearing scripture today, if you could create the cloud-like feeling of the mountaintop in the sanctuary. Dry ice could be placed in a tub behind the altar, and right before the service drizzle water on top of it. It may need more water poured over it as the service continues. Renting a smoke machine might be preferable. Reading the scripture with smoke in

the sanctuary would be very effective. Use Matthew 17:1-9 and 1 Peter 1:16-21. You could also use the Exodus passage to give background. The Matthew passage is one that could be acted out, but I think that would detract from the seriousness of the message.

Call to Offering
Today we are celebrating mountaintop experiences. Let us remember the times in our lives when we have been overcome with the awesomeness of God, and give generously so that others may have the opportunity to meet Christ.

Prayer of Dedication
The Psalmist tells us that God is a lover of justice, has established equity, and has executed justice and righteousness. May our offerings today go to help others who know neither justice nor equity. Gracious God, accept our meager gifts in the name of Jesus. Amen.

Benediction
Leader: Be as attentive to what you have heard and seen as to a lamp shining in a dark place, until the day dawns and the morning star rises in your hearts.
People: God said, "This is my Son, my Beloved, with whom I am well pleased."
Leader: May your hearts be filled with the glory of this wonderful news.
People: Our hearts are overflowing; we will tell of the glory of Jesus Christ.
Leader: Let us go to the mountain with Jesus. Amen.

Ash Wednesday

Joel 2:1-2, 12-17 or Isaiah 58:1-12 **Psalm 51:1-17**
2 Corinthians 5:20b—6:10 **Matthew 6:1-6, 16-21**

Hymns
Break Forth, O Beauteous (CBH203, PH26, UM223, NCH140)
Have Thine Own Way (CBH504, UM382)
The Sacrifice You Accept (CBH141)
Psalm 51 (PH196)
Dust And Ashes Touch Our Face (NCH186)
O For A Closer Walk With God (PH396, 397, NCH450)
Lord, Who Throughout These Forty Days (UM269, PH81, NCH211)
Forty Days And Forty Nights (PH77, NCH205)
Prayer Is The Soul's Sincere Desire (CBH572, NCH508)

Anthems
Change My Heart O God, Espinosa, *Lift Up Your Hearts*, p. 61
Lord, I Lift My Soul To You, Hopson, CGA, 2-part Mixed
For Things That I Do Wrong, Lord, Bedford, CGA, Unison, optional handbells
Create In Me A Clean Heart, O God, Carl Mueller, G. Shirmer, SATB

Call to Worship (based on Joel)
Leader: Blow the trumpet in Zion; sound the alarm on my holy mountain! Let all the inhabitants of the land tremble, for the day of the Lord is coming; it is near.
People: A day of darkness and gloom, a day of clouds and thick darkness!
Leader: Yet even now, says our God, return to me with all your heart, with fasting, with weeping, and with mourning;
People: A day of darkness and gloom, a day of clouds and thick darkness!
Leader: Rend your hearts and not your clothing. Return to Yahweh, who is gracious and merciful, slow to anger, and abounding in steadfast love.
People: Blow the trumpet in Zion; sanctify a fast; call a solemn assembly;
All: The day of salvation is at hand, it is near.

Call to Confession
Day after day we seek God and struggle to know God's path toward righteousness. Let us join together to pray to our God as we confess together.

Prayer of Confession
Gracious God, on this first day of Lent we gather to confess our sins and repent of our wrongdoings. On this day we come to humble ourselves, to bow down our heads and put ashes on our foreheads to be reminded of the great gift of Jesus Christ. But we are unable to hold the fast. When we see the hungry, we do not feed them; we know of the oppression of peoples, but we do very little. In fact, sometimes we just get tired of hearing about the homeless and the poor. Help us, God, to know that we must never cease in trying to bring justice and peace to the world in which we live. Help us spend less time on things that bring us wealth and power, and more time on trying to live a useful and purposeful life. Guide us, and make us strong in your love. Amen.

Assurance of Pardon
Isaiah tells us: "Yahweh will guide you continually, and satisfy your needs in parched places, and make your bones strong; and you shall be like a watered garden, like a spring of water, whose waters never fail." God, you gave us your beloved son to keep our garden fresh and new. We know that Jesus is our salvation. Amen.

Scripture Readings
Psalm 51:1-17: *This psalm can be found in the* Presbyterian Hymnal *as a responsive song. Have one of your good solo voices teach the response to the whole congregation, and then act as a cantor, singing this psalm. Explain to your congregation that this way of singing psalms may have been how Jesus listened to scripture in the temple.*

2 Corinthians 5:20b—6:10: *Have your regular liturgist begin the reading and read the passage through 6:4a — "but as servants of God we have commended ourselves in every way" — then have people in the congregation say the phrases listed. Have a different person for each phrase. They may remain seated, but they must speak out — they can have the phrases numbered on a piece of paper.*

    Through great endurance,
    In afflictions,
    Hardships,
    Calamities,
    Beatings,
    Imprisonments,
    Riots,
    Labors,
    Sleepless nights,
    Hunger,
    By purity,
    Knowledge,
    Patience,
    Kindness,
    Holiness of spirit,
    Genuine love,
    Truthful speech,
    And the power of God,
    With the weapons of righteousness for the right hand and for the left,
    In honor and dishonor,
    In ill repute and good repute.

Then have the liturgist finish the rest of the passage, beginning with v. 6:8b — "We are treated as imposters...."

Mark 6:1-6, 16-21: *This passage is part of the Sermon on the Mount. Have someone dressed as Jesus read this passage from the floor of the sanctuary, exactly as if he was on the hillside teaching. Walk through the congregation, stopping to look in people's eyes — telling them one thing, and then moving to someone else — coming back to the front to finish verses 6:19-21.*

Benediction

Leader: Go out into the world with ashes on your forehead. Wear them as a sign to others of your faith in your God.
People: We wear them as a sign of God's love for us.
Leader: When people say, "Your face is dirty," say,
People: Those are ashes. We wear them to remember that God loved us, and God loves you.
Leader: God sent his only son into the world so that we might be saved. Spread the word.
People: We will remember and go to serve others. Amen.

First Sunday In Lent

Genesis 2:15-17; 3:1-7   **Psalm 32**
Romans 5:12-19   **Matthew 4:1-11**

The Lenten Season
The lectionary passages for Lent in Cycle A are full of wonderful stories. A theme for the season might be "Stories of Struggle, Stories of Faith," and your services could revolve around the stories. Most of them can be dramatically interpreted, and this is a good way for children and youth to be included in worship. I have rewritten some of them for you. Read them over and think about who might be willing to participate in this retelling of the story. Each of you has a sanctuary which is unique, so I will ask you to use your own knowledge to ascertain where the people might stand. I will make suggestions, but you will have to alter them to fit your space. Some of these stories are powerful enough to stand alone, so do not "over-preach" after them. Enhance them — don't retell them.

Hymns
Today We Are All Called To Be (PH434)
God Marked A Line And Told The Sea (PH283, NCH568)
How Blest Are Those (PH132)
In The Stillness Of The Evening (CBH551)
Joys Are Flowing Like A River (CBH301, NCH284)
Spirit Of God, Descend Upon My Heart (CBH502, NCH290, UM500)
Lord Who Throughout These Forty Days (PH81, UM269, NCH211)
O Love, How Deep (PH83, NCH209, UM267)
I Am Leaning On The Lord (CBH532, UM416)
Our Father, Which Art In Heaven (PH589, UM271)

Anthems
Sing, Dance, Clap Your Hands, Ziegenhals
A Lenten Prayer, Powell
The Temptation Of Christ, Pfautsch, SLawson-Gould, SAT
The Lord's Prayer
Prayers, John Horman

The theme of the scripture passages for today is temptation and sinfulness — giving in to temptation.

Call to Worship
Leader: Be glad in God and rejoice, O righteous, and shout for joy, all you upright in heart.
People: We rejoice in God, and thank God in great humility.
Leader: God is mighty and gracious in forgiveness.
People: We rejoice in God, and thank God in great humility.
Leader: Let us worship God.
People: We come before our God with thanksgiving.

Call to Confession
Just as sin came into the world through one person, and death came through sin, so we continue to sin even as we struggle to follow Jesus. Let us come before God to confess and ask for forgiveness.

Prayer of Confession
Merciful God, on this first Sunday in Lent we are reminded of Jesus in the desert. He was tempted over and over again, and yet stayed steadfast in his goodness. We are tempted continually as we live our lives. We struggle with petty jealousies in the work world. We strive to be good parents and good children, but we are tempted by the world in which we live. We want material goods and a sense of power that no one needs. God, be with us in our struggle as you were with your son in the desert. Help us to be open to your leading and to your word as our example. Give us strength to stay on the upward path. And when we do stray, remind us that you will grant us forgiveness if we repent and turn to you. This we ask in the name of the Christ. Amen.

Assurance of Forgiveness
Just as by one person's disobedience the many were made sinners, so by one man's obedience the many will be made righteous. In the name of Jesus Christ, we are forgiven. Amen.

Scripture Readings
Genesis 2:15-17; 3:1-7; Matthew 4:1-11: *Use the Genesis passage about Adam and Eve in the garden and the Matthew passage concerning the temptation of Jesus. Both are great stories and take us from the first sin to Jesus' strength in rebuking sin. This would be a great Sunday to have a storyteller simply tell the stories. These are also stories children can understand to a degree, and it might be good to have two Sunday school classes rewrite them and interpret them in the light of today. The Genesis story could become a reality television show where the participants are on a desert island and may eat anything or go anywhere, except for this one restaurant, which supposedly serves incredible food and has the clues to winning the game. And Jesus could go to Los Angeles to be tempted by fame, power, clothes, makeovers, and so on.*

Or you could simply have a group of older children or youth act out the two scripture passages as written. All would get the point — we are all tempted, but God can help us to stay on the right path — and when we go astray Jesus is our guide to goodness and redemption.

Pastoral Prayer
Creative and loving God, we thank you for creating the incredible world in which we live. Each day as we go out into this world, we are caught up in its complexity. The sun's warmth, the dew on the grass, the power of a thunderstorm, and the playfulness of your creatures draw us in. How wonderful it would be if we could simply live in this world and enjoy it. But instead we barely take notice of it as we hurry to our cars or to the school bus to rush off to work or school. We say to ourselves, "This weekend we will spend with those we love and do something together outside." But far too often the weekend gets by us as well. If we're outside at all, it's to watch our children play soccer, and then rush off to another child's activity. We look at your great creation through a pane of safety glass. We are simply an anonymous person in our car, getting mad at another anonymous person who is in a bigger hurry than are we. We are often tempted to cut that person off or yell an obscenity, knowing we can get away with it. Our temptations are different than Jesus', but also the same. They have to do with the search for

power, the desire to protect ourselves and our loved ones, and our desire to be safe in a scary world. We think about what we can do to make our world a better place, but we really don't have time to do anything. Besides, we're just one person — what can we do? Help us to remember that what we can do is to follow you. We can study what is written in the Bible. We can follow the model of Jesus as he says, "Get behind me, Satan!" For it is written, "Worship the Lord your God, and serve only God." We can remember to love our neighbor as ourselves. Don't give up on us, God. Help us during this Lenten season to remember that we are your people; give us courage to "walk the walk" with you. Amen.

Benediction
Leader: Go out into the world as if you are going into the wilderness.
People: We go with Jesus as our guide.
Leader: Take strength in your faith, and stay steady.
People: We go with Jesus as our guide.
Leader: Open yourselves and allow the Holy Spirit to show you the way through all temptation.
People: Our hearts are open and we lift our eyes to God. Amen.

Second Sunday In Lent

Genesis 12:1-4a
Romans 4:1-5, 13-17
Psalm 121
John 3:1-17 or Matthew 17:1-9

Hymns
The God Of Abraham Praise (NCH24, UM116, PH488)
Unto The Hills We Lift (NCH466, CBH169, PH234)
Sing Praise To God, Who Reigns Above (PH483, UM126)
God Our Author And Creator (NCH530)
Dearest Jesus, We Are Here (PH493)
Like The Murmur Of The Dove's Song (PH314, UM544)
Christ Upon The Mountain Peak (CBH232, UM260, PH74)
O Wondrous Light, O Vision Fair (NCH184, UM258, PH75)

Anthems
I Will Lift Up Mine Eyes, Leo Sowerby, H. W. Gray
Lenten Meditation, Paul McKleen, handbells
Over All/Sobre Todos, Michael Jothen
God So Loved The World, John Horman

The theme found in scripture is "faith" — faith in God when you cannot understand what is being asked of you.

Call to Worship
Leader: Yahweh told Abram to leave his own country and go where God asked of him.
People: *(Singing)* The God of Abraham praise, all praised be his name.
Leader: I will make of you a great nation, and I will bless you, make your name great, so you will be a blessing.
People: *(Singing)* Who was and is and is to be and still the same.
Leader: So Abram went, as the Lord had told him.
People: *(Singing)* The one eternal God, the one that now appears.
Leader: Let us worship the God of Abram.
People: *(Singing)* The first, the last, beyond all thought, for timeless years.

Opening Hymn
The God Of Abraham Praise

Prayer of Invocation
Gracious God, give us the faith of Abraham, who didn't ask "why" when you told him to leave his home. Give us faith to "go where you send us," and do what you ask of us, and even to be able just to hear what you are telling us. Help us in this time of worship to open our eyes, ears, heart, and mind to your Word, so that our faith may be increased. Help us to be faithful people so that the promise you have given us may rest on grace, that we may be benefactors of your grace in Jesus Christ. Amen.

Scripture Readings
Genesis 12:1-4a; Romans 4:1-5, 13-17; John 3:1-17: *Read Genesis 12:1-4a to set the mood for the theme of faith — a reminder of what Abraham did. Then read Romans 4:1-5, 13-17. It is confusing but helps reiterate what Abraham did. Finish with John 3:1-17, and do this as a conversation between Nicodemus and Jesus. Props would consist of a table with two chairs, or simply a couple of comfortable low chairs, depending on what can be seen in your sanctuary. Possible script:*

Narrator: Now there was a Pharisee named Nicodemus, a leader of the Jews. *(Nicodemus might be wearing a clerical collar and all black)* He came to Jesus *(Dressed to look like himself)* by night — so as to not be seen — *(The two men sit down)* and said to him.

Nicodemus: Rabbi, we know that you are a teacher who has come from God; for no one can do these signs that you do apart from the presence of God.

Jesus: Truly, I tell you, no one can see the kingdom of God without being born from above.

Nicodemus: *(Looks amazed and confused)* How can anyone be born after having grown old? Can one enter into his mother's womb and be born a second time?

Jesus: I tell you that no one can enter the kingdom of God without being born of water and Spirit. What is born of the flesh is flesh, and what is born of the spirit is spirit. *(Nicodemus gets up and walks away from Jesus, looking really confused)* Don't be amazed that I said to you, "You must be born from above." *(Jesus gets up and follows Nicodemus, puts a hand on his shoulder)* The wind blows where it chooses, and you hear the sound of it, but you don't know where it comes from or where it goes. So it is with everyone who is born of the Spirit.

Nicodemus: *(To Jesus, with amazement)* How can these things be?

Jesus: *(Becoming a little impatient)* Are you a teacher of Israel, and yet you do not understand these things? I tell you, we speak of what we know and testify to what we have seen; yet you do not receive our testimony. If I have told you about earthly things and you don't believe, how can you believe if I tell you about heavenly things? No one has ascended into heaven except the one who descended from heaven, the Son of Man. And just as Moses lifted up the serpent in the wilderness, so must the Son of Man be lifted up, that whoever believes in him may have eternal life. *(Puts arm around shoulder of Nicodemus)* For God so loved the world that he gave his only Son, so that everyone who believes in him may not perish but may have eternal life. *(The two of them begin walking down the center aisle)* God did not send the Son into the world to condemn the world, but in order that the world might be saved through him. *(Go out of the sanctuary)*

Call to Offering
I lift my eyes to the hills — from where will my help come? Our help comes from the Lord, who made heaven and earth. Generously may we give back of what we earn to our God who is our help.

Prayer of Dedication
O God, the psalmist tells us that you are our keeper. So much of the world needs our help. Help us to work at your right hand to keep the world at peace. May our gifts today be used to achieve your goals. In Jesus' name we pray. Amen.

Benediction (based on Psalm 121)
Leader: The Lord is your keeper; Yahweh is your shade at your right hand.
People: The sun shall not strike us by day, or the moon by night.
Leader: Yahweh will keep you from all evil; he will keep your life.
People: Yahweh will keep our going out and our coming in from this time on and forevermore. Amen.

Third Sunday In Lent

Exodus 17:1-7   Psalm 95
Romans 5:1-11   John 4:5-42

Hymns
I Hunger And I Thirst (CBH474)
Let's Sing Unto The Lord (CBH55, UM149)
What Wondrous Love Is This (CBH530, PH85, UM292)
Creator God, Creating Still (NCH278)
Glorious Things Of Thee Are Spoken (PH446, UM731)
Soul, Adorn Thyself With Gladness (CBH473)
I Heard The Voice Of Jesus Say (CBH493)
Fill My Cup, Lord (UM641)

Anthems
Desert Song, Robert Kreutz, SATB
Look Around!, Helen Kemp, Unison/2-part
Two Rainstick Pieces, Hubert, CG

Call to Worship (based on Psalm 95)
Leader: Come, let us sing to our God. Let us make a joyful noise to the rock of our salvation.
People: Let us come into God's presence with thanksgiving; let us make a joyful noise to God with songs of praise!
Leader: Come, let us worship and bow down, let us kneel before God, our Creator.
People: For we are the people of God's pasture, and the sheep of God's hand. We come today to listen for God's voice.

Call to Confession
We say that God is our rock and redeemer, but we often don't act like we believe it. Let us come before God during this Lenten season, pouring our hearts out together. Let us pray.

Prayer of Confession
Loving and faithful God, don't you get tired of us calling out to you, "We're thirsty. Give us a drink. We need more. We're worried. Are you really there? Prove it — give us what we think we need and what we want." Forgive us, God. We are a fearful people — and there is so much of which to be afraid. There's war, and the economy, and people out there who don't look or act like us. They frighten us. Sometimes we then frighten those we love because we're so frightened. Help us, God. Show us the way, and help us to know that you are steadfast in your love for us and faithful in your everlasting presence. Give us courage to face our demons, whatever and wherever they may be. Amen.

Assurance of Forgiveness
In his letter to the Romans, Paul says, "Since we are justified by faith, we have peace with God through our Lord Jesus Christ. For while we were still weak, at the right time Christ died for the ungodly. God proves his love for us in that while we still were sinners Christ died for us." Alleluia! We are forgiven. Amen.

Scripture Readings
Exodus 17:1-7 and John 4:5-42 have the commonality of the phrase, "Give me a drink of water," and the theme of people thirsting for God and yet not trusting. Both passages lend themselves well to story. The Exodus passage may be read as a litany between a Narrator, Moses, Yahweh, and the Congregation. The John passage is perfect to be presented as drama.

Exodus 17:1-7
Pastor or Narrator: From the wilderness of Sin the whole congregation of the Israelites journeyed by stages, as Yahweh commanded. They camped at Rephidim, but there was no water for the people to drink. The people quarreled with Moses, and said,

Congregation: Give us water to drink.

Narrator: Moses said to them,

Moses: *(Dressed in biblical costume, standing in the middle of the main aisle)* Why do you quarrel with me? Why do you test Yahweh?

Narrator: But the people thirsted there for water,

Women: We thirst.

Children/Youth: We're thirsty.

Narrator: And the people complained against Moses and said,

Men: Why did you bring us out of Egypt, to kill us and our children and livestock with thirst?

Narrator: So Moses cried out to Yahweh,

Moses: What shall I do with this people? They are almost ready to stone me.

Narrator: Yahweh said to Moses,

Yahweh: *(Standing behind altar in contemporary clothing)* Go on ahead of the people, and take some of the elders of Israel with you; *(Moses asks leaders of the congregation to join him and begins moving forward to chancel area, carrying a staff)* take in your hand the staff with which you struck the Nile, and go. I will be standing there in front of you on the rock at Horeb. Strike the rock, and water will come out of it, so that the people may drink. *(Moses hits large rock in center of chancel)*

Narrator: Moses did so, in the sight of the elders of Israel. He called the place Massah and Meribah, because the Israelites quarreled and tested Yahweh, saying,

Congregation: Is Yahweh among us or not?

John 4:5-42

Leave large rock in center of chancel. Move well (with sign on it, "Jacob's Well," perhaps created by the children) next to large rock. Characters: Jesus, several Disciples, Samaritan Woman, eight to ten Samaritans, sitting in the middle of the congregation.

(Jesus comes up to well, looking hot and tired, and sits down on the rock. After a few seconds Samaritan woman comes with a water jar to draw water. She does not look at Jesus)

Jesus: Give me a drink.

Samaritan Woman: *(Looks up in surprise, and then back down)* Why are you asking me, a woman from Samaria, for a drink? Jews and Samaritans don't like each other.

Jesus: If you knew the gift of God, and who it is that is saying to you, "Give me a drink," you would have asked him, and he would have given you living water.

Samaritan Woman: *(Astonished)* Sir, you have no bucket, and the well is deep. Where do you get that "living" water? Are you greater than our ancestor Jacob *(Points to sign)*, who gave us the well, and with his sons drank from it?

Jesus: Everyone who drinks of this water here will be thirsty again, but those who drink of the water I will give them will never be thirsty. The water I will give will become in them a spring of water gushing up to eternal life.

Samaritan Woman: Sir, give me this water, so that I'll never be thirsty or have to keep coming here in the middle of the day to draw water.

Jesus: Go get your husband, and then come back here.

Samaritan Woman: *(Looking embarrassed)* I have no husband.

Jesus: You are right in saying, "I have no husband"; for you have had five husbands, the one you have now is not your husband. What you have said is true.

Samaritan Woman: Sir, I see that you are a prophet. Our ancestors worshiped on this mountain, but you say that the place where people must worship is in Jerusalem.

Jesus: *(Stands up)* Woman, believe me, the hour is coming when you will worship the Father neither on this mountain nor in Jerusalem. You worship what you do not know; we worship what we know, for salvation is from the Jews. *(Comes out closer to the congregation)* But the hour is coming, and is now here, when the true worshipers will worship the Father in spirit and truth, for the Father seeks such as these to worship him. For God is spirit *(Turns back toward woman)*, and those who worship him must worship in spirit and truth.

Samaritan Woman: I know that the Messiah is coming. When he comes, he will proclaim all things to us.

Jesus: I am he, the one who is speaking to you.

(Disciples come up side aisle and see Jesus talking to a woman. Hurrying toward him, they are astonished, but say nothing. Woman leaves her water jar and moves down the center aisle to the center of congregation. Puts hand on several people as if to get them to come with her. She is excited)

Samaritan Woman: Come and see a man who told me everything I have ever done! He cannot be the Messiah, can he? *(Several people get up and go with her back up aisle slowly)*

Disciples: *(Offering bread)* Rabbi, eat something.

Jesus: *(Shakes head no)* I have food to eat that you do not know about.

Disciples: *(Looking at each other)* Surely no one has brought him something to eat?

Jesus: My food is to do the will of him who sent me and to complete his work. Do you not say, "Four months more, then comes the harvest?" *(Samaritans gather around, listening)* I tell you, look around you, and see how the fields are ripe for harvesting. The reaper is already receiving wages and is gathering fruit for eternal life, so that sower and reaper may rejoice together. For here the saying holds true, "One sows and another reaps." I sent you to reap that for which you did not labor. Others have labored, and you have entered into their labor.

One Samaritan: I believe in him because of what the woman told me.

Other Samaritans: Come, stay with us for a few days.

Second Samaritan: I believe in him because of what he tells us.

(Jesus and Disciples exit down center aisle)

Third Samaritan: *(Speaks to Samaritan Woman)* Now it is no longer because of what you said that we believe, for we have heard for ourselves, and we know that this is truly the Savior of the whole world.

Benediction
Leader: God is your rock, and your salvation.
People: God keeps us from stumbling in our going out and coming in.
Leader: God be with you till we meet again.
People: We go with God, filled with reverence and joy.

Fourth Sunday In Lent

1 Samuel 16:1-13   **Psalm 23**
Ephesians 5:8-14   **John 9:1-41**

Hymns
God Of The Prophets (NCH358)
Gentle Shepherd (CBH352)
The Lord's My Shepherd (PH170, UM136, CBH578)
The King Of Love (PH171, UM138, CBH170)
My Shepherd Will Supply My Need (PH172, CBH589)
Savior, Like A Shepherd Lead Us (PH387, CBH355, UM381)
He Leadeth Me (UM128, CBH599)
Shepherd Me, O God (CBH519)
This Little Light Of Mine (CBH401, UM585)
Amazing Grace (PH280, UM378)
All Who Love And Serve Your City (PH413, UM433)
Jesus The Christ Says (NCH48)

Anthems
Do You Know Your Shepherds Voice?, Lord 2-part
Walk As Children Of The Light, Kallman, Morningstar, SATB
A Lenten Prayer, Powell, CGA, Unison, Flute
The King Of Love My Shepherd Is, CGA 904, various voicings

Call to Worship
Leader: For once you were darkness, but now in the Lord you are light. Live as children of light.
People: For the fruit of the light is found in all that is good and right and true.
Leader: The Lord is my shepherd; I shall not want.
People: God leads me beside still waters. God restores my soul.
Leader: Let us worship God and be comforted.

Prayer of Invocation
God our Shepherd, we come to you to be comforted and reassured. But we also come to be challenged to change our lives. Help us, on this fourth Sunday in Lent to hear your word spoken and interpreted so that even though we walk through a dark valley, we can really fear no evil — knowing that you are with us. Help us to dwell in your house forever more. Amen.

Scripture Readings
Samuel 16:1-13; John 9:1-41: *The two wonderful stories offered us this week are from 1 Samuel 16:1-13 (Samuel anointing David), and John 9:1-41 (Jesus healing the blind man). Use a storyteller to retell the 1 Samuel story. There are too many people in this story to try to dramatize it any other way. It would be best if the person could memorize it, but a well-prepared reading can work. The John passage is perfect for dramatization using a mixture of children, youth, and adults.*

John 9:1-41

Characters include Jesus, three to four Disciples, Blind Man, four to five Neighbors, four Pharisees, and Blind Man's Parents. All are dressed in biblical costumes except for the Pharisees who are in long, flowing robes, like judges or ministers.

(Jesus enters left with Disciples and walks toward Blind Man who is sitting off center, perhaps in front of the pulpit. Blind man might be begging. Jesus and disciples stop, noticing the man)

Disciples 1 and 2: Rabbi, who sinned, this man or his parents that he was born blind?

Jesus: Neither this man nor his parents sinned: He was born blind so that God's works might be revealed in him. We must work the works of him who sent me while it is day; night is coming when no one can work. As long as I am in the world, I am the light of the world. *(Leans over and spits on the ground, makes mud with the saliva, and spreads mud on Blind Man's eyes)* Go, wash in the pool of Siloam. *(Jesus and Disciples go on across stage and wait in the wings. Blind Man goes behind pulpit and comes back able to see)*

Blind Man: I can see! I can see!

(Neighbors, scattered on the chancel, begin coming over to see what has happened)

Neighbor 1: Is this not the man who used to sit and beg?

Neighbor 2: Yes, that's him.

Neighbor 3: No, that's not him — it's just someone who looks like him.

Blind Man: I am the one.

Neighbors 4 and 5: Then how were your eyes opened?

Blind Man: The man called Jesus made mud, spread it on my eyes, and said to me, "Go to Siloam and wash." Then I went and washed and received my sight.

All Neighbors: *(Looking around)* Where is he?

Blind Man: *(Looking around)* I don't know.

(Neighbors grab Blind Man and take him to Pharisees who are lurking up close to altar or communion table)

Neighbor 1: This man says Jesus healed him today — the Sabbath.

Pharisees: What happened to you?

Blind Man: Jesus put mud on my eyes. Then I washed, and now I see.

Pharisees 1 and 2: *(Speaking haughtily)* This man is not from God, for he does not observe the Sabbath.

Pharisee 3: But how can a man who is a sinner perform such signs?

(All Pharisees argue with each other, then two turn one way and two turn the other way)

Pharisee 4: *(Turns and speaks again to the blind man — others turn back to hear)* What do you say about him? It was your eyes he opened.

Blind Man: He is a prophet.

Pharisee 1: I don't believe he really was ever blind.

Pharisee 2: Let's have his parents brought to us, and ask them.

(A neighbor gets parents)

Pharisee 3: Is this your son, who you say was born blind? How then can he see?

Blind Man's Parents: We know that this is our son, and that he was born blind ...

Blind Man's Father: We do not know how it is that he can now see.

Blind Man's Mother: Nor do we know who opened his eyes.

Blind Man's Parents: Ask him; he's of age. He can speak for himself. *(Turning to each other, the father says to the mother in a stage whisper)* I'm not telling them I think Jesus did it. They could throw us out of the synagogue. *(Mother agrees. Both turn back to Pharisees)* Ask him. He is of age. *(Blind Man's Parents leave right)*

Pharisee 4: *(Turning back to the Blind Man)* Give glory to God! We know that the man who healed you is a sinner.

Blind Man: I do not know whether he is a sinner. One thing I do know — I was blind and now I see.

Pharisees 1 and 2: What did he do to you?

Pharisee 3: How did he open your eyes?

Blind Man: I already told you, and you won't listen. Why do you want me to tell you again? Do you want to become his disciples, too?

Pharisees: You are his disciple, but we are disciples of Moses.

Pharisee 4: We know that God has spoken to Moses, but as for this man, we don't know where he comes from.

Blind Man: This is an astonishing thing! You do not know where he comes from — and yet he opened my eyes. We know that God doesn't listen to sinners, but he listens to one who worships him and obeys his will. Never since the world began has it been heard that anyone opened the eyes of a person born blind. If this man were not from God, he could do nothing.

Pharisee 1: *(Practically screaming at Blind Man)* You were born entirely in sin, and you are trying to teach us. Get out! Get out!

(Blind Man goes back to sit by the pulpit. Neighbor 2 goes over to tell Jesus what has happened. Jesus walks over to Blind Man)

Jesus: Do you believe in the Son of Man?

Blind Man: And who is he, sir? Tell me, so that I may believe in him.

Jesus: You have seen him, and the one speaking with you is he.

Blind Man: Lord, I believe. *(Blind man falls at Jesus' feet. Pharisees sneak over to hear what is being said)*

Jesus: I came into this world for judgment so that those who do not see may see, and those who do see may become blind.

Pharisee 2: Surely we aren't blind, are we?

Jesus: If you were blind, you would not have sin. But now that you say, "We see," your sin remains.

(Jesus, Disciples, and some Neighbors walk off one way, Pharisees and other half of Neighbors go off the other, leaving only the Blind Man. As congregation sings Amazing Grace, *Blind Man slowly walks down center aisle, looking at everyone, and leaves)*

Benediction
Leader: God does not see as mortals see. God does not look on the outward appearance.
People: God looks into our hearts
Leader: God wants us to go into the world spreading the love of Jesus Christ. Look into the hearts of all whom you meet.
People: We go into the world with our eyes opened. We can now see. Amen.

Fifth Sunday In Lent

Ezekiel 37:1-14   **Psalm 130**
Romans 8:6-11   **John 11:1-45**

Hymns
Let It Breathe On Me (NCH288)
Out Of The Depths, O God, We Call (NCH554)
Out Of The Depths I Cry To You (UM515)
O Spirit Of God (NCH60)
Why Has God Forsaken Me? (CBH246, PH406)
When Jesus Wept (NCH192, CBH234, PH312)
I Greet You, Sure Redeemer (NCH251)
I Am The Bread Of Life (CBH472)

Anthems
My Song Is Love Unknown, Jennings
I Want Jesus To Walk With Me, arr. Hopson, 2-part with trombone
Refresh My Heart, Lord, Bullock, Maranatha! *Praise Band 7*
Jesu, Joy Of Man's Desiring, J. S. Bach/Donald Allured, National, 4 to 5-octave handbells

Call to Worship (based on Psalm 130)
Leader: Wait for the Lord! My soul waits, and in his word I hope.
Women: My soul waits for the Lord more than those who watch for the morning.
Men: More than those who watch for the morning.
Leader: O Israel, hope in the Lord!
Women: For with the Lord there is steadfast love,
Men: With God is great power to redeem.
All: It is God who will redeem us from all our iniquities. Let us worship God.

Call to Confession
Out of the depths we call to you, God. God, hear our voices — be attentive to the voice of our supplication as we confess our sins together.

Prayer of Confession
Mighty God, we worry so much. No matter how much we try we cannot be like the lilies of the field. We worry about our health, our work, our families, and our possessions. Help us to know that you are with us. We know that you are our help in times of trouble. But we want control of our lives. We want to know that the things we do will keep us safe and make us happy. Forgive us, God, for not trusting you. We don't understand that your steadfast love is our happiness. Help us to trust in your saving grace, given freely through Jesus Christ, our savior. Amen.

Assurance of Forgiveness
In Romans 8, Paul assures us: "To set the mind on the flesh is death, but to set the mind on the Spirit is life and peace. If the Spirit of God who raised Jesus from the dead dwells in you, this God will give life to your mortal bodies also through God's Spirit that dwells in you." Hallelujah! We are forgiven. Amen.

Scripture Readings
Ezekiel 37:1-14; Psalm 130; Romans 8:6-11; John 11:1-45: *All four of the scripture readings for today are about new life in God. The Ezekiel passage is best done by one person playing Ezekiel — retelling this conversation and amazing feat. It should be done from the floor of the sanctuary and memorized. It would be especially meaningful if the person playing Ezekiel were dressed as a desert prophet. Psalm 130 and the Romans passage have been used in the prayers for today. John 11:1-45 is very long, but is a particularly dramatic passage and could be well told as drama. It could be read by one person and pantomimed by the cast of characters — Mary, Martha, Messenger, Jesus, several Disciples, Thomas, several Mourners, Lazarus. The Narrator must be able to read with great impact, slowing up for the pantomiming to be effective. A good hymn to be sung after the reading would be* When Jesus Wept.

Call to Offering
God, there is so much sadness in the world. May our offerings go to bring joy to the despondent and new life to people without hope. Let us be generous in our giving.

Prayer of Dedication
Generous and loving God, you give us life abundant. Bless our gifts that they may help those who suffer in darkness. May these gifts bring new light to the world. Amen.

Benediction
Leader: God says, "I will put my Spirit in you, and you shall live."
People: We live to go with God.
Leader: Peace be with you as you leave this place.
People: We leave, renewed in spirit, to do God's work in the world.
Leader: Go with God. Amen.

Palm Sunday/Sunday Of The Passion
Sixth Sunday In Lent

Isaiah 50:4-9a   Psalm 31:9-16
Philippians 2:5-11   Matthew 21:1-11 or Matthew 26:14—27:66

Hymns
At The Name Of Jesus (PH148, UM168, CBH342)
All Hail The Power Of Jesus' Name (PH142, 143, CBH106, NCH304)
He Is Lord (UM177)
Blessed Be The Tie That Binds (CBH421)
Go To Dark Gethsemane (PH97, CBH240)
He Never Said A Mumblin' Word (PH85)
Hosanna, Loud Hosanna (UM27, PH89, NCH213)
Mantos y Palmas/Filled With Excitement (UM279, NCH214)
All Glory, Laud, And Honor (PH90, NCH216)

Anthems
Hosanna, Loud Hosanna, Kenyon, Agape, handbells
Let This Mind Be In You, Claussen, Mark Foster, SATB
Into Jerusalem, Taranto, CGA, Unison
God So Loved The World, Horman, CGA, Unison/2-part, optional flute/violin

Begin the service with much festivity, having children and families proceeding down the aisle waving palms and shouting Hosanna during the opening hymn (suggestion Hosanna! Loud Hosanna*). It shows the fleeting joy of Christ's entrance into Jerusalem. The day then would become more somber.*

Call to Worship
Leader: "Hosanna! Loud Hosanna," the little children sang.
People: Blessed be the Son of David!
Leader: At the name of Jesus, every knee shall bow; everyone confess him King of Glory now!
People: We will never deny you, Jesus. We bow before you and worship you.
All: Hosanna! Save us!

Call to Confession
As we enter into Holy Week, a week where Jesus shows us every human emotion, let us come together to confess our own weaknesses before our God. Let us pray.

Prayer of Confession
God, we come together today both to celebrate Jesus' triumphant entry into Jerusalem, and to prepare ourselves for Jesus' trial, conviction, crucifixion, and burial. It is a week full of emotion. We wonder how those who knew and loved Jesus best could possibly deny, betray, and desert him. But deep down we know how: they were human, and let fear get the best of them. We do that, too, God — every day. We know that you love us, but sometimes you seem so far

away. Where are you, God? Even your son called out to you — and yet he knew that your plan called for this. What is your plan for us, God? Help us to take deep breaths when we are anxious, and turn our lives over to you. This we ask in the name of Jesus, for whom every knee shall bow. Amen.

Assurance of Forgiveness
Christ Jesus, who, though he was in the form of God, emptied himself, being born in human likeness. He humbled himself and became obedient to the point of death on a cross. Therefore God highly exalted him and gave him the name that is above all names. Let us bow before our redeemer, knowing that we are forgiven. Hosanna in the highest!

Scripture Readings
Matthew 21:1-11; Matthew 26:14—27:66: *These readings from the Gospel of Matthew would be appropriate. The first is Matthew 21:1-11 to remind us of the triumphal entry in Jerusalem when everyone believes Jesus to be the long-awaited Messiah. The other passage is excerpts from the lectionary passage, Matthew 26:14—27:66. Much of this passage will be retold on Maundy Thursday and Good Friday. Concentrate today on the betrayal passages. Have the following passages read by people sitting in the congregation. They would simply stand up, state the passage, and then read it in a somber voice. The congregation would then respond with, "Surely, not us, Jesus!" There should be at least thirty seconds of silence before the next selection. Matthew 26:14-16; 26:20-25; 26:30-34; 26:36-39; 26:40-46; and 26:47-50 are suggestions for the selections. After the reading, the choir might sing* O Love, How Deep *(PH83) as a response to the scripture.*

Congregational Prayer
Enfolding God, today is an emotional day. The people surrounding Jesus had such high hopes. They loved this man, and they believed him. Where did it suddenly go wrong? "I will never desert you, Lord!" they told him. Yet he knew. He knew, and he loved them anyway. He loved them enough to commit the ultimate sacrifice for them. We love you, too, Jesus. And we also betray you. Thank you for your continuing love, no matter how far we wander from the path. Thank you, God, for giving us the greatest gift — your child. We know how it is to lose a loved one or to see one suffer. Today we come to you, offering up the names of those we love who are suffering with grief, pain, and illness. Be with them as you were with Jesus. He never quit praying. Help us to pray, also. Today we pray for the leaders of the world. Give them courage and confidence to do only those things which bring peace and healing.

God, today we ask for wisdom to do your will in our daily lives. Help us to keep before us the model of Jesus in his own life — a life of kindness to others, of justice to all he met, and of telling the good news of God's love to all he met. This we ask in the name of our mentor and redeemer, Jesus Christ, who taught his disciples to pray together. (Our Father, who art in heaven....)

Benediction
Leader: We trust in you, O God.
People: We say, "You are our God."
Leader: Our times are in your hands.
People: Let your face shine upon us.
All: Save us in your steadfast love. Amen.

Maundy Thursday

Exodus 12:1-4 (5-10) 11-14   Psalm 116:1-2, 12-19
1 Corinthians 11:23-26   John 13:1-17, 31b-35

Hymns
I Love The Lord, Who Heard My Cry (PH362, NCH511)
More Love To Thee, O Christ (PH359)
Lord, You Give The Great Commission (PH429)
Eat This Bread (CBH471)
Bread Of The World (CBH469, PH502)
For The Bread Which You Have Broken (UM615)
Christ At Table There With Friend (NCH227)
Jesu, Jesu, Fill Us With Your Love (PH367, NCH498, UM432)
An Upper Room Did Our Lord Prepare (PH94)
Jesus, Thou Joy Of Loving Hearts (PH510, 511)

Anthems
Love One Another, Hopson, CGA, Unison 2-part
Don't Listen To The Hammer Ring
Pan de Vida, Hurd, OCP, 3-part
Angels, Bear My Soul Away, Cornell

The following is an alternative to the normal Maundy Thursday service. The service begins at 6:30 p.m. with a simple soup supper — members bring a pot of soup or loaves of bread to share. The evening is intended to be intergenerational — children six and up can participate in the entire experience. Childcare can be provided for younger children after the meal has ended. The bulletin might look like this:

Maundy Thursday

We Approach God

Welcome and Introductions

Call to Worship and Grace
Leader: I love Yahweh, who has heard my voice and my supplications.
People: Because Yahweh listened, I will call on Yahweh as long as I live.
Leader: What shall we return to Yahweh for all this bounty?
People: We will lift up the cup of salvation and call on the name of Yahweh.
Leader: We will offer to Yahweh a thanksgiving sacrifice.
All: Praise God forever.

(A light supper of soup and bread is now shared with all)

Hymns   *What Wondrous Love Is This*
                                              An Upper Room Did Our Lord Prepare

We Encounter God and Our Humanity

Old Testament Reading — Exodus 12:1-14
New Testament Reading — John 13:1-17, 31b-35

Journey through Holy Week — 7:30 p.m.
Spend time working individually at centers experiencing the Holy Week events through poetry, art, music, journaling, and meditation. There will be ten centers from which to choose. Visit one or several — work at your own pace — spend time with the story.

For more information on how to create spirituality centers, order the resource "Centering on the Spirit — A Resource for Setting Up a Spirituality Center," by Carl Horton. PDS #70-250-02-107. Presbyterian Distribution Center, 888-728-7228, ext. 5460.

We Respond to God and Our World

Service of Holy Communion (in the sanctuary) — 8:30 p.m.

Invitation to Communion

Hymn — *Jesus, Thou Joy Of Loving Hearts*

Communion Prayer

Lord's Prayer

Words of Institution

Communion

Communion Anthem

Prayer of Thanksgiving

Benediction

Pastor: On the night before he died, to the government betrayed, at his people's freedom meal, Jesus broke the bread, and said,
People: "Take and eat my broken self. Share in all I say and do. Though I go, I shall return: God is making all things new."
Pastor: When the meal was nearly done, and his blood would soon be shed, Jesus lifted up the cup, "All must drink of this," he said,
People: "When the powers of earth prevail and my blood is shed for you, taste the sign within the wine: God is making all things new."
Pastor: Go in peace to love and serve our God.
All: Amen.

Please leave the sanctuary in silence.

Good Friday

Isaiah 52:13—53:12 Psalm 22
Hebrews 10:16-25 or Hebrews 4:14-16; 5:7-9 John 18:1—19:42

Hymns
Deep Were His Wounds And Red (PH78)
What Wondrous Love Is This (PH85, NCH223, UM292)
Santo, Santo, Santo (CBH400, UM65)
Ah, Holy Jesus (CBH254, NCH218, PH93, UM289)
Why Has God Forsaken Me? (CBH246, PH168)
I Am Thine, O Lord (UM419)
My Song is Love Unknown (NCH222, PH76)
Were You There? (NCH229, PH102, UM288)
O Sacred Head (PH98, UM286, NCH226)
He Never Said A Mumbalin' Word (PH95)
Calvary (PH97)

Anthems
The Walk To Calvary, N. Anderson
From the *Messiah: He Was Despised*, G. F. Handel
When I Survey The Wondrous Cross, Hall Hopson, Lorenz, handbells

Call to Worship (based on Psalm 22)
Leader: You who are in awe of Yahweh, praise God! Glorify and stand in awe, you offspring of Israel!
People: Yahweh hears us when we cry out in fear.
Leader: The poor shall eat and be satisfied. Those who seek shall praise Yahweh. May your hearts live forever!
People: All the ends of the earth shall remember and turn to God, and all the families of the nations shall worship before our God.
Leader: Future generations will be told the story,
People: And proclaim deliverance to a people yet unborn by Yahweh's sacrifice.
Leader: Let us worship and praise the Lord.

Opening Hymn
What Wondrous Love Is This

Call to Confession
Today we come to hear the story of the last hours of Jesus' life. It is a tragic story, one we'd rather not hear. We bring to this story our own sinfulness and our own rejection of our God — even as we call ourselves Christians. Let us pray now as one body, confessing our sinfulness.

Prayer of Confession
Merciful God, what a day this must have been for you — watching your own son — despised, reviled, mocked, and even killed so that we mortals might be saved from ourselves. We come

together to be reminded of Jesus' sacrifice and your mercy. Forgive us, God, for forgetting your love for us, for denying the enormity of the sacrifice, for acting like we deserved this kind of sacrifice in the first place. Forgive us for putting ourselves ahead of you and your desires for us. We are a selfish people who must constantly be reminded of your love and generosity. Don't give up on us, we pray.

Assurance of Forgiveness (based on Hebrews 10:16-22)
This is the covenant which I will make of them, says the Lord: I will set my laws in their hearts and write them on their understanding; and their sins and wicked deeds I will remember no more at all. And where these have been forgiven, there are offerings for sin no longer. So now, my friends, the blood of Jesus makes us free to enter boldly into the sanctuary by the new, living way, which he has opened for us through the curtain, the way of his flesh. We have, moreover, a great priest set over the household of God; so let us make our approach in sincerity of heart, and full assurance of faith, our guilty hearts sprinkled clean, our bodies washed with pure water.

Scripture Readings and Music
This is a perfect service to let scripture stand alone — accentuated with music — no sermon is needed. The reading choir and congregational singing is interspersed with the dramatizational readings.

Isaiah 52:13—53:5
Two readers alternate verses
First reader — a young person twelve to thirteen years old
Second reader — older man in his '50s to '60s with distinguished voice
He was Despised, from Handel's *Messiah*, performed by choir or soloist

Isaiah 53:6-9
Woman of any age
All We Like Sheep, from Handel's *Messiah*, performed by the choir

Isaiah 53:10-12
Same woman
Ah, Holy Jesus, performed by congregation

John 18:1-12
Narrator — young woman
Jesus — man in early '30s
They — a small group (four or five people)
Go to Dark Gethsemane, performed by congregation

John 18:13-27
Narrator — can be same or different
Jesus — same
Peter — any age or sex (each time Peter denies Jesus, he moves to another place in the sanctuary)
They — 3 different people confronting Peter (can be sitting in sanctuary close to where Peter is standing)
Once, Twice, A Third Time from *If these Stones Could Speak*, Keithahn/Horman, Abingdon, performed by choir (can be sung as a round)

John 18:28—19:1
Narrator
Jesus
Pilate — any age man
They
He Was Despised performed by soloist

John 19:2-15
Narrator
2 Soldiers
Pilate
They
Jesus
O Sacred Head, Now Wounded, performed by choir and congregation

John 19:16-22
Narrator
They
Pilate
He Was Despised performed by soloist

John 19:23-27
Narrator
Soldiers
Jesus
Mary
John
At the Cross, Her Vigil Keeping performed by congregation

John 19:28-30
Narrator
Jesus
Were You There? performed by a soloist and congregation

John 19:31-37
Narrator
He Was Despised performed by choir or soloist

John 19:38-42
Narrator
When I Survey The Wondrous Cross performed by handbells or congregation

Benediction
No benediction is used. Congregation simply leaves in silence — nothing is finished.

The Resurrection Of Our Lord/Easter Day

Acts 10:34-43 or Jeremiah 31:1-6 **Psalm 118:1-2, 14-24**
Colossians 3:1-4 or Acts 10:34-43 **John 20:1-18 or Matthew 28:1-10**

Hymns
Thine (Yours) Is the Glory (NCH253, PH122, CBH269)
Hail To The Lord's Anointed (CBH185)
O Day Of Radiant Gladness (PH470)
This Is The Day (NCH84, UM657)
Rejoice, The Lord Is King! (CBH288)
Jesus Christ Is Risen Today (NCH240)
Celebrate With Joy And Singing (PH107)
The Strife Is O'er (CBH263)
Come Ye Faithful, Raise The Strain! (CBH264, 265)

Anthems
The Whole World Sings Alleluia, Wayne Wold, CGA, Unison
Let Us Rejoice And Sing, Schultz, Unison/2-part
Easter Morning, Paul Christiansen, SATB, Augsburg Fortress
Alleluia, Randall Thompson, SATB, Schirmer
Easter selections from *Messiah,* G. F. Handel
An Easter Festival, Sharon Rogers, Lorenz, 2 to 3-octave handbells

Before the service begins, have the sanctuary decorated with lilies and other flowers, but the altar or communion table should be empty except for a pile of white linen cloths.

Call to Worship (based on Psalm 118)
Leader: Open the gates of righteousness, that we may enter through them and give thanks to God.
People: This is the gate of God, the righteous shall enter through it.
Leader: Thanks be to God for answering us and becoming our salvation.
People: This is God's doing, it is marvelous in our eyes.
Leader: Alleluia, Christ is risen!
People: Christ is risen, indeed!

Opening Hymn
Thine (Yours) Is The Glory

Prayer of Thanksgiving
Jubilant and all-powerful God, we give you great thanks for this glorious day. Death has been swallowed up in victory. As we recount the events of Christ's resurrection, give us ears to hear this ancient story with new commitment. Help us to walk beside the risen Christ in our daily lives. May we truly rejoice at this incredible news. Alleluia! May we shout it out to the whole world! Amen.

Scripture Readings

Acts 10:34-43: *Have someone in the congregation be Peter preaching to the congregation as he did long ago. It would be best if he could memorize the part and say it in "first person."*

John 20:1-18: *Have a narrator tell the story while it is acted out. Have the different characters say their own lines. Have the altar or communion table be the tomb where Jesus had lain. It is now empty except for white linens lying on it in two places — at the head and in the middle.*

Narrator: Early on the first day of the week, while it was still dark, Mary Magdalene came to the tomb and saw that the stone had been removed from the tomb. *(Mary Magdalene comes in from one side. She sees the tomb [altar or communion table] and looks amazed and frightened, with her hands on her face. She turns and runs up the middle aisle where two Disciples are waiting near the back of center aisle)* So she ran and went to Simon Peter and the other disciple, the one whom Jesus loved, and said to them,

Mary: They have taken the Lord out of the tomb, and we do not know where they have laid him.

Narrator: Then Peter and the other disciple set out and went toward the tomb. *(Two Disciples begin hurrying up aisle toward table. Mary is about three steps behind them. She stops at base of steps to the nave)* The two were running together, but the other disciple outran Peter and reached the tomb first. *(One Disciple stops about three feet from table, and notices linen wrappings)* He looked in and saw the linen wrappings lying there, but he did not go in. Then Simon Peter came *(Peter walks past other disciple and stops at table)*, and went up to the tomb. He saw the linen wrappings lying there *(Peter touch cloths in middle of table)*, and the cloth that had been on Jesus' head, not lying with the linen wrappings but rolled up in a place by itself. *(Peter touch cloths at head of table)* Then the other disciple came up to the tomb, and he saw and believed. *(Disciple 1 joins Peter behind table. They look at each other incredulously and bow heads)* For as yet they did not understand the scripture, that he must rise from the dead. Then the disciples returned to their homes. *(Disciples leave off toward right. Mary now comes up steps and walks to the table)* But Mary stood weeping outside the tomb. As she wept, she went to look in the tomb. *(Two angels come from each side and take their places at each end of the table)* And she saw two angels in white, standing where the body of Jesus had been lying, one at the head and the other at the feet. They said to her:

Angels: Woman, why are you weeping?

Mary Magdalene: *(Very sadly)* They have taken away my Lord, and I do not know where they have laid him. *(Jesus comes out and stands about three feet away from the table in front of it)*

Narrator: When she had said this, she turned around *(Mary turns to leave)* and saw Jesus standing there, but she did not know that it was Jesus.

Jesus: Woman, why are you weeping? Who are you looking for?

Narrator: Supposing him to be the gardener, she said to him,

Mary: Sir, if you have carried him away *(Looks around frantically)*, tell me where you have laid him, and I will take him away.

Jesus: Mary!

Mary: Rabbouni! Teacher! *(Starts to throw her arms around Jesus or grab his hand. Jesus puts hand out to stop her from touching him. Angels leave, go off to each side)*

Jesus: Do not hold on to me, because I have not yet ascended to the Father. But go to my brothers and say to them, "I am ascending to my Father and your Father, to my God and your God."

(Mary turns, and walks out to edge of steps or in front of congregation)

Mary: *(Speaks to whole congregation)* I have seen the Lord!

(Jesus walks off to right. Mary walks right down the center aisle, looking at different folk saying, "I have seen the Lord" quietly)

Hymn
Christ The Lord Is Ris'n Today
(During the singing of this hymn, women will come up the middle aisle with flowers, a cross, and candles to place on the table. Remove the white cloths when the women depart)

Call to Offering
Peter said that God shows no partiality, but loves all people. Jesus of Nazareth healed all who were oppressed. May our offering today serve all people as they hear the good news of salvation. The ushers will now wait upon us for the morning offering.

Prayer of Dedication
"Christ has risen! Shout hosanna! Celebrate this days of days!" God, bless these gifts joyfully given to honor you and the Risen Christ. May this offering serve people who need it, no matter their happenstance in life, and may they find peace of mind in you. Amen.

Benediction
Leader: The strife is o'er, the battle done. The victory o'er death is won.
People: But the battle for a godly, peaceful life continues.
Leader: Go with joy and fortitude to live as the Risen Christ would have us live.
People: We go, believing anew in the love and graciousness of a caring God.
All: Share the good news! Christ is risen! Alleluia!

Second Sunday Of Easter

Acts 2:14a, 22-32 **Psalm 16**
1 Peter 1:3-9 **John 20:19-31**

Hymns
I Danced In The Morning (UM261, PH 302)
Christ Is Risen! Shout Hosanna! (CBH 272)
Jesus, The Very Thought Of Thee (NCH507)
We Live By Faith And Not By Sight (NCH256, PH398)
O Sons And Daughters, Let Us Sing (NCH244, PH116, 117)
Breathe On Me, Breath Of God (CBH356, UM420, PH316)
These Things Did Thomas Count (NCH284)
When In The Night I Meditate (PH165)

Anthems
From the *Messiah: I Know That My Redeemer Liveth*, G. F. Handel
Perfect Love, Jane Marshall, TTBB, Hinshaw
Jesus, Son Of God Most High, Cox and Lindh, CGA, Unison/2-part
Share The Easter Joy, Patterson, Unison/2-part with handbells

Call to Worship (based on Psalm 16)
Leader: Yahweh is our chosen portion and our cup; you hold us in your hand.
People: We bless Yahweh who gives us counsel; in the night also our hearts instruct us.
Leader: We keep Yahweh always before us; because God is at our right hands, we shall not be moved.
People: Therefore our hearts are glad, and our souls rejoice; our bodies also rest secure.
All: You show us the paths of life. In your presence there is fullness of joy. In your hand are pleasures forevermore. Blessed be our God.

Call to Confession
Protect us, O God, for in you we take refuge. We say to Yahweh, "You are my God, I have no good apart from you." In all humility let us come before God confessing our sins together.

Prayer of Confession
Merciful and loving God, you know us so well. How disappointed we must make you. It has been only seven days since we celebrated the resurrection of your beloved Son. Have we already forgotten? We try so hard to believe, but we are like Thomas. We need a sign — or some proof that we can touch or see or hear. Help us, O God, to just simply believe. Help us to quiet the noise of the outside world which says, "I need proof," and simply rest in you. Keep the fire in our hearts for faithfulness to burn on. Help us to say with joy, "My Lord and my God." Amen.

Assurance of Forgiveness
Blessed be the God and Parent of our Lord Jesus Christ! By great mercy God has given us a new birth into a living hope, through the resurrection of Jesus Christ from the dead! By your belief you receive the outcome of your faith — the salvation of your souls. In Jesus Christ we are forgiven.

Scripture Readings
1 Peter 1:3-9: *This passage could be read by someone dressed as Peter. Have him come forward from the congregation, beginning by introducing himself using the first two verses of the chapter. In most countries other than the United States, Christian congregations begin their services by saying something like: "Grace to you and peace in the name of Jesus Christ, our Lord and Savior." Here is a suggestion for the beginning: "I am Peter, Apostle of Jesus Christ, speaking to God's scattered people who lodge for a while in Pontus, Galatia, Cappadocia, Asia, and Bithynia — chosen of old in the purpose of God, hallowed to God's service by the Holy Spirit, and consecrated with the sprinkled blood of Jesus Christ. Grace and peace to you in fullest measure." Then he would read the passage directly from the Bible, or have it on a scroll from which he could read it, or have it memorized.*

John 20:19-31: *Older children or youth could easily act out this passage. Use both boys and girls as disciples — Cast: Narrator, Ten Disciples, Thomas, and Jesus.*

(Ten Disciples come from different places in the sanctuary. The first two pretend to unlock a door next to the pulpit, and come in stealthily, looking around them. Close door behind them. Rest of Disciples come in groups of two to three, knock on pulpit until someone lets them in. All should look nervous and worried. The Disciples will greet each other with a hug or handshake, looking as if they are glad to see each other)

Narrator: When it was evening on the first day of the week, and the doors of the house where the disciples had met were locked for fear of the Jewish leaders, Jesus came and stood among them.

Jesus: *(Stands up from behind the pulpit and moves into the middle of Disciples while they are greeting each other)* Peace be with you. *(Holds out hands and point to side)*

Disciples: It is you, Master! *(Drop to knees and look overjoyed)*

Jesus: Peace be with you. As the Father has sent me, so I send you. *(Blows breath on each of them as they kneel)* Receive the Holy Spirit. If you forgive the sins of any, they are forgiven them; if you retain the sins of any, they are retained. *(Jesus then goes back behind the pulpit. Disciples get up and start talking to each other quietly)*

(Thomas comes to pulpit and knocks)

Narrator: But Thomas (who was called the Twin), one of the twelve was not with them when Jesus came. *(A Disciple opens the door and lets him in. He is hugged with joy)*

Disciples: We have seen the Lord!

Thomas: *(Shakes head negatively with vigor)* Unless I see the mark of the nails in his hands, and put my finger in the mark of the nails in his hands, and my hand in his side, I will not believe. *(All Disciples turn their back on the congregation and remain still)*

Narrator: A week later his disciples were again in the house, and Thomas was among them. *(Disciples turn around in twos and threes and act like they are in conversation with each other)* Although the doors were shut, Jesus came *(Jesus comes up from behind the pulpit and moves to the middle of the Disciples)* and stood among them.

Jesus: Peace be with you. *(Turns to Thomas)* Put your finger here and see my hands. *(Points to palm of hand. Then points to side)* Reach out your hand and put it in my side. Do not doubt but believe.

Thomas: My Lord and my God! *(Gets on knees)*

Jesus: Have you believed because you have seen me? Blessed are those who have not seen and yet have come to believe. *(Turns and looks at all Disciples. All walk off and return to their seats)*

Narrator: Now Jesus did many other signs in the presence of his disciples, which are not written in this book. But these are written so that you may come to believe that Jesus is the Messiah, the Son of God, and that through believing you may have life in his name. The gospel of our Lord Jesus Christ.

Congregation: Thanks be to God.

Benediction
Leader: Jesus asks us: "Have you believed because you have seen? Blessed are those who have not seen and yet have come to believe."
People: Help us to believe by faith alone.
Leader: Go into the world and seek Jesus in the faces of the people you meet. Believe and be joyful.
People: Help us to be more like Jesus in all that we do and say.
All: Our Lord and our God! Alleluia! Amen.

Third Sunday Of Easter

Acts 2:14a, 36-41
1 Peter 1:17-23
Psalm 116:1-4, 12-19
Luke 24:13-35

Hymns
I Want To Be Ready (NCH616)
I Love My God, Who Heard My Cry (NCH511, PH362)
Jesus, Priceless Treasure (NCH480)
O Lamb Of God, Most Holy (PH82)
Abide With Me (NCH99, CBH653, UM700)
Be Known To Us In Breaking Bread (NCH342, PH505)
There Is A Place Of Quiet Rest (CBH5)
Break Thou The Bread Of Life (CBH361)

Anthems
See That You Love One Another, Joseph Roff, H. W. Gray, SATB/Soprano solo
Open Our Eyes, Lord, Bob Cull, *Worship And Praise*
Lord, Make Me An Instrument Of Thy Peace, Lindh, SATB
In Thee Is Gladness, Cherwien, Unison or SATB

Call to Worship (based on Psalm 116)
Leader: I love the Lord, because he has heard my voice and my supplications.
People: Because God inclined his ear to me, therefore I will call on God as long as I live.
Leader: What shall I return to God for all gifts to me?
People: I will lift up the cup of salvation and call on the name of Yahweh.
Leader: I will pay my vows to Yahweh in the presence of all people,
All: In the courts of the house of Yahweh, in your midst, O Jerusalem. Praise God!

Call to Confession
"There is a place of quiet rest near to the heart of God." Let us take our remorse and fears to God by offering our Prayer of Confession, first together and then individually and silently. Let us pray.

Prayer of Confession
Gracious God, how often have we not recognized you in the midst of us? When we meet together as a congregation to make decisions about the mission of this church, do we recognize you? Or do we take sides — afraid to listen to others because something around here might change? Are we so afraid that something or someone might be different that we refuse to see you? Or are we so afraid that we might become stagnant that we cannot hear what people love about this place? Come unto us and open our eyes to see you here. Help us to look for you, God. Forgive us for only being concerned about ourselves and for not looking to see how we can most effectively bring others in to your house. This we ask in the name of Jesus, the Christ. Amen.

Assurance of Forgiveness (based on 1 Peter 1:17-23)
Hear the good news! Through Jesus' model we have come to trust in God, who raised him from the dead and gave him glory. You have been born anew, not of perishable but of imperishable seed, through the living and enduring word of God.

Scripture Readings
Acts 2:14a, 36-41: *The Acts passage is again a speech by Peter, this time at Pentecost. It would be good if the person playing Peter could memorize this passage. At the end of verse 39, another person might read verses 40-41.*

Luke 24:13-35: *This is another good story to be dramatized. Ask some of your young adults to dramatize this passage. There are four characters: Narrator, two Followers — Cleopas and Other — and Jesus. Two persons are walking up the center aisle. Have Jesus sit about six rows back, on the center aisle.*

Narrator: Now on that same day two of them were going to a village called Emmaus, about seven miles from Jerusalem, and talking with each other about all these things that had happened. While they were talking and discussing, Jesus himself came near and went with them, but their eyes were kept from recognizing him.

Jesus: *(Stands and joins Followers)* What are you discussing with each other while you walk along? *(Cleopas and Other stop and look very sad)*

Cleopas: Are you the only stranger in Jerusalem who does not know the things that have taken place there in these days?

Jesus: What things?

Other: The things about Jesus of Nazareth, who was a prophet mighty in deed and word before God and all the people.

Cleopas: And how our chief priests and leaders handed him over to be condemned to death and crucified him.

Other: But we had hoped that he was the one to redeem Israel.

Cleopas: Yes, and besides all this, it is now the third day since these things took place.

Other: Moreover, some women of our group astounded us. They were at the tomb early this morning.

Cleopas: And when they did not find his body there, they came back and told us that they had indeed seen a vision of angels who said that he was alive.

Other: Some of those who were with us went to the tomb and found it just as the women had said; but they did not see him.

Jesus: Oh, how foolish you are, and how slow of heart to believe all that the prophets have declared! Was it not necessary that the Messiah should suffer these things and then enter into his glory? *(The three of them begin walking again, but do not go up onto the nave)*

Narrator: Then beginning with Moses and all the prophets, he interpreted to them the things about himself in all the scriptures. As they came near the village to which they were going, Jesus walked ahead as if he were going on. *(Followers stop, Jesus goes ahead)*

Cleopas and Other: Wait. Stay with us, because it is almost evening and the day is nearly over.

Jesus: All right. *(Three walk to altar where there is a loaf of bread. Jesus breaks the loaf, bows head, and then hands bread to the two)*

Narrator: When he was at the table with them, he took bread, blessed and broke it, and gave it to them. Then their eyes were opened, and they recognized him; and he vanished from their sight. *(Jesus walks off)*

Cleopas: Were not our hearts burning within us while he was talking to us on the road, while he opened the scriptures to us?

Other: It was incredible! *(Walks down the steps of chancel with Cleopas)*

Narrator: That same hour they got up and returned to Jerusalem; and they found the eleven and their companions gathered together.

Cleopas: *(Says to congregation)* The Lord has risen indeed!

Other: He has appeared to Simon!

Narrator: Then they told what had happened on the road, and how he had been made known to them in the breaking of the bread.

All Three: The gospel of our Lord Jesus Christ.

Congregation: Thanks be to God.

Closing Hymn
Open Our Eyes, That I May See

Benediction
Leader: Jesus is with us, even when our eyes are closed to him.
People: God, open our eyes that we might see.
Leader: Jesus talks with us even when we aren't listening
People: Open our ears that we might hear.
Leader: Jesus listens to us and teaches us.
People: Open our mouths that we might tell of the great deeds of our Savior.
Leader: Go into the world making disciples of those who have not heard.
All: Spirit Divine!

Fourth Sunday Of Easter

Acts 2:42-47　　　　　　Psalm 23
1 Peter 2:19-25　　　　　John 10:1-10

Hymns
Let Us Break Bread Together (NCH330, CBH618)
He Leadeth Me (CBH128)
My Shepherd Is The Living God (NCH247)
The King Of Love, My Shepherd Is (CBH170, UM138)
Savior, Like A Shepherd Lead Us (CBH355, UM381, PH387)
I Bind My Heart This Tide (CBH411)
Thuma Mina (CBH434)
You Satisfy The Hungry Heart (UM629)

Anthems
The Lord Is My Shepherd, John Rutter, Oxford, SATB
Savior, Like A Shepherd Lead Us, Linda McKechnie, Agape, 3-ocave handbells
Do You Know Your Shepherd's Voice?, Wayne Lord, CGA, 2-part
I'm The Good Shepherd, Barta, 2-part

Call to Worship
Leader: Who is the Good Shepherd?
People: Christ is our Good Shepherd.
Leader: The Lord is my shepherd; I shall not want.
People: He makes me lie down in green pastures; he leads me beside still waters.
Leader: Jesus tells us he is the gate of the sheepfold. Whoever enters by him shall be saved, and will come in and go out and find pasture.
People: The Lord is my sheep gate; I shall not want.
All: Let us worship God.

Prayer of Invocation
Dear God, on this Fourth Sunday of Easter, we come to you filled with the story of Christ's love. We look to the image of the early Christians, some of whom experienced Jesus' ministry; others simply heard about his love for all. We gather today to learn about Jesus' sacrificial nature — he described himself as the Good Shepherd, the Gate of the Sheepfold, the protector of God's creatures. Open us up to receive fresh meaning from ancient stories, so that we can adapt our own lives to that of modern-day shepherds. In Jesus' name we pray. Amen.

Scripture Readings
Psalm 23: *Read this Psalm as a congregational litany. People love the words of this psalm and many know it by heart from the King James Version. Use that version if you like — it is very poetic.*

1 Peter 1:19-25: *This passage is a call to bravery for the early Christians — reminding them of Jesus' bravery and sacrifice. "No sacrifice is too great." It ends with a reminder of Jesus as shepherd.*

John 10:1-10: *This passage is from a teaching of Jesus. It could be read by two people — Narrator and Jesus; or it could be read by a choral speaking choir. I would put them in a V-shape such as this:*

```
        E
     D     F
    C       G
    B       H
    A       I
```

Voices A and I: Very truly, I tell you, anyone who does not enter the sheepfold by the gate but climbs in by another way is a thief and a bandit.

Voice B: The one who enters by the gate is the shepherd of the sheep.

Voice H: The gatekeeper opens the gate for him, and the sheep hear his voice. He calls his own sheep by name and leads them out.

Voices C and G: When he has brought out all his own, he goes ahead of them, and the sheep follow him because they know his voice.

All: They will not follow a stranger, but they will run from him because they do not know the voice of strangers.

Voice E: Jesus used this figure of speech with them, but they did not understand what he was saying to them.

Voice D: So again Jesus said to them, "Very truly, I tell you, I am the gate for the sheep.

Voice F: All who came before me are thieves and bandits; but the sheep did not listen to them.

Voice A: I am the gate.

Voice I: Whoever enters by me will be saved, and will come in and go out and find pasture.

Voices B and H: The thief comes only to steal and kill and destroy.

All: I came that they may have life, and have it abundantly."

Voice E: The gospel of our Lord, Jesus Christ.

Congregation: Thanks be to God.

Call to Offering
The book of Acts tells us that the early Christians would sell their possessions and distribute the proceeds to all, as any had need. Let us remember that kind of communal giving as we proceed with our own offering collection today. The ushers will now wait upon us.

Prayer of Dedication
All-knowing God, we thank you for all your wonderful gifts to us throughout history. We appreciate all the sacrifices of your people, from the ancient Israelites to the early Christians, for the Reformation to the Pilgrims. May the gifts we bring today be used to help people who need your help. Help us as Christians in the twenty-first century to help others know your love. In Jesus' name we pray. Amen.

Benediction
Leader: Savior, like a shepherd lead us; we really need your tender care.
People: In your pleasant pastures feed us; for our use your sheepfolds prepare.
Leader: Blessed Jesus, you have bought us; we are yours.
People: Blessed Jesus, you have loved us; love us still. Amen

Fifth Sunday Of Easter

Acts 7:55-60 Psalm 31:1-5, 15-16
1 Peter 2:2-10 John 14:1-14

Hymns
In You, Lord, I Have Put My Trust (PH183)
Christ Is Made The Sure Foundation (NCH400, UM559, PH416, 417)
Christ Is Our Cornerstone (CBH43)
Come, O Spirit, Dwell Among Us (PH129)
O Jesus, I Have Promised (NCH493)
Here, O God, Your Servants Gather (NCH72, CHB7, PH465)
Hallelujah! What A Savior (UM165)
Come, My Way, My Truth, My Life (NCH331)

Anthems
Step By Step, Worship And Praise, 132
When Stephen Full Of Power And Grace, Richard Peck, H. W. Gray, SATB
Dear Lord, Lead Me Day By Day, Jane Marshall, Unison
Celebrate The Good News, Tom Mitchell, CGA, 2-part

Call to Worship
Leader: You are a chosen race,
Men: A royal priesthood,
Women: A holy nation
All: God's own people,
Leader: In order that you may proclaim the mighty acts of him who called you out of darkness
People: Into his marvelous light.
Leader: Once you were not a people,
People: But now we are God's people;
Leader: Once you had not received mercy,
People: But now we have received mercy.
All: Let us worship God.

Call to Confession
Do not let your hearts be troubled. Believe in God. Let us bring our confessions before the God who loves us. Let us pray.

Prayer of Confession
Wonderful God, we come to you today confessing our confusion over your word. We don't read the Bible very often, and we know we should. It offers us insight into what you would have us do in our everyday living. But sometimes the scripture passages are very difficult, and other times they are confusing. We read them and say, "What does this have to do with life in the twenty-first century?" or, "I just don't believe that Jesus meant to say that." Help us, God, to continue to find great meaning in this Holy Book. Forgive our doubts. Open our ears to hear

what you would have us hear. Give us new confidence that you are talking to us through this ancient book. Help us to hear the stories with new energy, seeking wisdom in its pages. Amen.

Assurance of Pardon
Hear the good news! Jesus came to save us from our sins. What a great gift we have been given. Alleluia! Amen.

Scripture Readings
1 Peter 2:2-10: *Have a choral speaking choir say this 1 Peter passage. Have each member of the choir hold a stone about the size of a fist. As they read the passage have members place a stone on the altar or communion table during the reading of verses 4, 5, 6, 7, 8 — every time the word "stone" is mentioned. The stones could be flat so that they could be placed like an "Ebenezer," or if they are more round, just placed together. The rest of the decorations might include a larger rock (perhaps one of the lightweight, fake rocks about two feet tall), flowers, and a small church.*

John 14:1-14: *This passage is a discussion between Jesus and his followers. Three members of the choral speaking choir might step forward from the rest and have this conversation. It would be important that they memorize their lines. The speakers would be Jesus, Thomas, and Philip. Leave out the phrases "Jesus said to him," "Thomas said to him," and so on.*

Call to Offering
God is our rock of refuge and our strong fortress. May our offering today help those around the world who need refuge and a strong fortress to protect them from war, hunger, and homelessness. The ushers will wait upon us for the morning offering.

Litany of Dedication
Leader: God is our rock
People: And our salvation.
Leader: Whom shall we fear?
People: Our fear is in our God, who has given us many blessings.
Leader: We offer these gifts to you, God. May they help others to know you, and find help in times of struggle.
People: We use these gifts in your name, our rock and our redeemer. Amen.

Benediction
Leader: The church's foundation is built upon God, the cornerstone.
People: We offer ourselves as a foundation of living stones.
Leader: Through your faith others can lean on you and begin their own faith journey.
People: Make us a cornerstone of faith. Christ is our cornerstone.
Leader. Have faith. Believe. Amen.

Sixth Sunday Of Easter

Acts 17:22-31 Psalm 66:8-20
1 Peter 3:13-22 John 14:15-21

Hymns
Our Cities Cry To You, O God (PH437)
Love Divine, All Loves Excelling (PH376, UM384, LBW315, NCH43)
Holy Spirit, Truth Divine (PH321, UM465)
There's A Sweet, Sweet Spirit (PH398, UM334)
Thy Holy Wings, O Savior (UM502)
Come Down, O Love Divine (LBW508, NCH289, PH313)
O Master, Let Me Walk With Thee (OBW492, NCH502, PH357)
My Song Is Love Unknown (LBW94, NCH222, PH76)

Anthems
Praise The Lord, Service Music, Hal Hopson, CGA, Unison 2-part
If You Love Me, Patterson, CGA, SAB, SATB
If Ye Love Me, Thomas Tallis, several publishers, many voicings
The Voice Of His Praise, Malcolm Williamson, Boosey and Hawkes, Unison/congregation

Call to Worship (based on Psalm 66)
Leader: Bless our God, O peoples; let the sound of God's praise be heard.
People: Come and hear, all you who fear God; and we will tell what God has done for us.
Leader: We cried aloud to Yahweh, and extolled God with our voices.
People: If we had cherished iniquity in our hearts, Yahweh would not have listened.
Leader: But truly God has listened; God has given heed to the words of our prayers.
All: Blessed be God, because our prayers have not been rejected and God's steadfast love is always with us. Let us worship God.

Call to Confession
Jesus tells us that he will not leave us orphaned, that he is coming to us. But sometimes we feel just like orphans, alone and unloved. Let us confess those sins that cause us to feel so alone. Let us pray.

Prayer of Confession
Loving and merciful God, why do we feel so alone in this world? We are surrounded by people every day, and yet we do not reach out. We stay wrapped up in our own world. Even those we love most do not receive our genuine love. We let the busyness of each day get in the way of our relationships. Jesus loved his disciples and was sorry to leave them. He wanted them to understand that he would be "with them" always. But they couldn't understand it, just as we find it so hard to understand that we are truly never alone. You are right there waiting for us to engage you in our lives. Help us, God. Keep our minds focused on you, and not the material things we can see. Help us to know that you will give us all we need. Jesus knew that, and we want to understand, also. Amen.

Assurance of Forgiveness
Hear the good news! Christ loves us, Christ suffered for sins once for all, the righteous for the unrighteous, in order to bring us to God. Christ was put to death in the flesh, but made alive in the Spirit. Christ loves us and forgives us. Alleluia!

Scripture Readings
Acts 17:22-31: *This is a perfect passage for one person to memorize and give just as Paul would have done it. Have someone introduce it by saying, "Paul is in Athens, waiting for Silas and Timothy to arrive. He is concerned because of all the idols he sees everywhere. Some of the philosophers brought him to the Areopagus, and asked him to tell them about this new teaching of Jesus. So Paul, standing in the middle of the Areopagus, said:" The person playing Paul would then stand directly in front of the congregation and recite this passage as if he were ready to engage in a debate.*

John 14:15-21: *This passage could be easily done by a small group of three people with a Narrator explaining that this passage is part of Jesus' explanation to his disciples of what is going to happen to him. He explains that he will not leave them alone. Begin with the speakers standing as shown below.*

2
1 3

Voice 2: If you love me, you will keep my commandments.

Voice 1: And I will ask the Father,

Voice 3: And he will give you another Advocate

All: To be with you forever.

Voice 1: This is the Spirit of truth, whom the world cannot receive, because it neither sees him nor knows him.

Voice 3: You know him, because he abides with you, and he will be in you.

All: I will not leave you orphaned; I am coming to you.

Voice 2: In a little while the world will no longer see me, but you will see me;

Voices 1 and 3: Because I love, you also will live.

Voice 2: On that day you will know that I am in my Father, and you in me, and I in you.

(Speakers move to new positions)

2
1
3

Voice 1: They who have my commandments and keep them are those who love me;

Voice 3: And those who love me will be loved by my Father

All: And I will love them and reveal myself to them.

Call to Offering
What God has prepared for those who love God will be revealed to us by the Holy Spirit. Let us prepare to share God's gifts with others by giving generously to the morning offering.

Prayer of Dedication
Gracious and loving God, we bring our gifts today because we want to help those who are less fortunate than ourselves. We have been given great gifts through your loving kindness, and we want those around the world to know that love. Accept our offering and use it to further your work, so that we might better understand the gifts you have bestowed on us. Amen.

Benediction
Leader: Go in peace, to do what is good and right in God's name.
People: May God go with us to guide us in our deeds.
Leader: God is with you always. It is we who remove ourselves from God.
People: Let us walk with God as we go through the coming week. Let us remember Jesus' model of ministry.
Leader: In the name of the God who created us, Jesus who loves us, and the Holy Spirit who spurs us on — Go in peace. Amen.

The Ascension Of Our Lord

Acts 1:1-11 Psalm 47 or Psalm 93
Ephesians 1:15-23 Luke 24:44-53

Hymns
Holy Spirit, Truth Divine (CBH 508, UM465)
Peoples, Clap Your Hands! (PH194)
A Hymn Of Glory, Let Us Sing (NCH259, PH141)
Rejoice, The Lord Is King! (CBH288, UM716, PH155)
Alleluia! Sing To Jesus! (PH144)
Hail, O Festal Day! (NCH262)
Spirit Divine, Inspire Our Prayers (CBH30, PH325)
Hail The Day That Sees Christ Rise (NCH260)

Anthems
People Of God, Rejoice!, Allen Pote, Hope Pub., SATB/handbells
God Has Gone Up, Titcomb, H. W. Gray, SATB
Sing To God, Butler, CGA, 2-part
Christ's Own Body, Margaret Tucker, 2-part

Call to Worship (based on Psalm 47)
Leader: Clap your hands, all you peoples;
People: Shout to God with loud songs of joy.
Leader: For God, the Most High, is awesome,
People: A great ruler over all the earth.
Leader: God has gone up with a shout,
People: Our God with the sound of a trumpet.
Leader: Sing praises to God, sing praises;
People: Sing praises to our marvelous God.
Leader: For God is ruler of all the earth;
All: Sing praises with a psalm.

Call to Confession
In the book of Acts, two angels asked Jesus' followers, "People of Galilee, why do you stand looking up toward heaven? This Jesus who has been taken up from you into heaven will come in the same way as you saw him go into heaven." Let us confess our sins of disbelief unto our God. Let us pray.

Prayer of Confession
O Great and glorious God, for whom all things are possible, why is it so hard for us to believe? We read the story of your ascension into heaven, and the first thing we want to say is, "Right. That sounds like complete fiction to us." But it isn't the words of the story that are important. What is important is our belief that, with you, all things are possible. All things.... Forgive us, God, for forgetting to pray when our life gets out of control. Forgive us for not knowing that you are right there, walking beside us, wanting to be part of our lives and our decision-making.

Forgive us for not talking to you about all aspects of our lives — the joyful, the discouraging, the bothersome, and the difficult. On this Ascension Sunday, help our unbelief. Amen.

Assurance of Forgiveness
In the Gospel of Luke, Jesus said, "Thus it is written, that the Messiah is to suffer and to rise from the dead on the third day, and that repentance and forgiveness of sins are to be proclaimed in his name to all nations." Brothers and sisters, through Jesus the Christ our sins are forgiven.

Scripture Readings
A choral speaking choir would work well for both these passages — with several solo voices.

Acts 1:10-11: *Have the choir stand in two rows with the soloists on the first row, something like this:*

```
        X X X X X X X X
        X X 1 3 4 2 X X
```

Voice 1: While staying with them, he ordered them not to leave Jerusalem, but to wait there for the promise of the Father.

Voice 2: "This," he said, "is what you have heard form me; for John baptized with water but you will be baptized with the Holy Spirit not many days from now."

Voice 1: So when they had come together, they asked him,

Speaking Choir: Lord, is this the time when you will be restored the kingdom to Israel?

Voice 2: He replied, "It is not for you to know the times or periods that the Father has set by his own authority. But you will receive power when the Holy Spirit has come upon you; and you will be my witnesses in Jerusalem, in all Judea and Samaria, and to the ends of the earth."

Speaking Choir: When he had said this, as they were watching, he was lifted up, and a cloud took him out of their sight. While he was going and they were gazing up toward heaven, suddenly two men in white robes stood by them.

Voices 3 and 4: They said, "Men of Galilee, why do you stand looking up toward heaven? This Jesus, who has been taken up from you into heaven, will come in the same way as you saw him go into heaven."

Luke 24:44-53: *Move the choir into a V-shape with the solo voice who is Jesus at the tip*

```
            X X X X
             X X X
              X X
               S
```

Choir: Then he said to them:

Solo: These are my words that I spoke to you while I was still with you — that everything written about me in the Law of Moses, the prophets, and the psalms must be fulfilled.

Choir: Then he opened their minds to understand the scriptures, and he said to them,

Solo: Thus it is written, that the Messiah is to suffer and to rise from the dead on the third day and that repentance and forgiveness of sins is to be proclaimed in his name to all nations, beginning from Jerusalem. You are witnesses of these things. And see, I am sending upon you what my Father promised; so stay here in the city until you have been clothed with power from on high.

Choir: Then he led them out as far as Bethany, and lifting up his hands, he blessed them. While he was blessing them, he withdrew from them and was carried up into heaven. And they worshiped him, and returned to Jerusalem with great joy; and they were continually in the temple blessing God.

Benediction (based on Ephesians 1:17-21)
Leader: May the God of our Lord Jesus Christ, the God of glory, give you a spirit of wisdom and revelation.
People: So that, with the eyes of our hearts enlightened, we may know what is the hope to which we have been called
Leader: That you may know the glorious inheritance among the saints and the immeasurable greatness of God's power for us who believe
People: Far above all rule and authority and power and dominion, and above every name that is named, not only in this age but also in the age to come. Amen.

Seventh Sunday Of Easter

Acts 1:6-14
1 Peter 4:12-14; 5:6-11
Psalm 68:1-10, 32-35
John 17:1-11

Hymns
Hail, O Festal Day (NCH262, UM324)
Holy Spirit, Truth Divine (CBH508, UM465)
God Of The Sparrow (NCH32, PH272, UM122)
Sing Praise To God Who Reigns Above (CBH59, PH483, UM126)
I'll Praise My Maker (CBH166, PH253, UM60)
O Love, How Vast, How Flowing Free (NCH209, PH83, UM267)
In Christ There Is No East Or West (CBH306, PH439, 440, UM548)
Born Of God, Eternal Savior (NCH542)

Anthems
Let God Arise, Eugene Butler, SMP, SATB
That They May All be One, Carl Mueller, G. Schirmer, SATB
O Sing To The Lord/Cantad al Senor, Ziegenhals, CBA, Unison/2-part
O Praise The Lord, Ye Children, Powell, 3-part

Call to Worship (based on Psalm 68)
Leader: Let the righteous be joyful; let them exult before God; let them be jubilant with joy.
Men: Sing to God, sing praises to God's name.
Women: Lift up a song to God who rides upon the clouds,
People: Be exultant before Yahweh,
Leader: Parent of orphans and protector of widows is God in the holy habitation.
People: Sing to God, O kingdoms of the earth; sing praises to the Holy One.

Call to Confession
Humble yourselves under the mighty hand of God, so that God may exalt you in due time. Cast all your anxiety on Yahweh, because you are cared for. Let us come together confessing our sins before the Almighty.

Prayer of Confession
Gracious God, since the dawn of our faith, Christians have always been persecuted somewhere, even today. Holy wars abound. But we're not persecuted ourselves in this place at this time. So why do we act that way sometimes? We do not live our faith with gratitude and awe. We have a hard time simply coming to church once a week, whereas the first Christians lived together and shared their belongings. We are selfish in our giving to the church, because there are so many material possessions that we just "have to have." Forgive us, God. Help us set our priorities by putting our faith first. Give us strength to proudly share our beliefs with others. Give us courage to let others know the great joy we have in loving you. Amen.

Assurance of Forgiveness
The God of all grace, who has called you to eternal glory in Christ, will restore, support, strengthen, and establish you. In Jesus Christ, we are forgiven.

Scripture Readings
Acts 1:6-14: *The Acts passage reminds us once again of the Ascension, and then goes on to name the disciples who have re-gathered in Jerusalem. It is also clear that there were women among them, as well as Jesus' mother and brothers. One liturgist or the pastor can simply read it.*

John 17:1-11: *This passage is part of a prayer Jesus says, asking for strength for what is to come — for himself and for his disciples. It is offered right before Jesus goes to the garden where he is arrested. It is a soliloquy, which would be very effective given by someone in a kneeling, prayerful position. It would be best memorized, but could be done with much practice in reading.*

Prayer of Dedication
Giving God, Jesus often prayed to you on behalf of the world, which he would be leaving. Jesus had great concern for people in the world, for their safety, their health, for their souls. May the gifts we have given today help the people of the world to be fed, housed, clothed, and to know Christ. Amen.

Benediction
Leader: May God bless you with joy and faith.
People: May we share all God's blessings with others.
Leader: May the love of Jesus go with you today.
People: May we share the love of Jesus with others.
Leader: May the Holy Spirit give you energy for the journey.
People: May it be so. Amen.

The Day Of Pentecost

Acts 2:1-21 or Numbers 11:24-30   Psalm 104:24-34, 35b
1 Corinthians 12:3b-13 or Acts 2:1-21   John 20:19-23 or John 7:37-39

Hymns
Holy Spirit, Truth Divine (CBH508, PH321)
Fire Of God, Undying Flame (NCH64)
Wind Who Makes All Winds That Blow (NCH271, CBH31, UM38, PH131)
Filled With The Spirit's Power (NCH266, CBH289, UM537)
Like The Murmur Of A Dove's Song (CBH29, UM544, PH314)
O Spirit Of The Living God (CBH361, UM539)
Spirit Of The Living God (PH322)
Many And Great, O God (NCH3, UM148, PH271)
I Sing The Mighty Power Of God (CBH46, UM152, PH288)
Forward Through The Ages (NCH277, UM555)
Breathe On Me, Breath Of God (CBH356, UM420, PH316)
Let It Breathe On Me (NCH288, UM503)
Glorious Things Of Thee Are Spoken (CBH619, UM731, PH446)

Anthems
Therefore, Give Us Love, Daniel Moe, Augsburg, 2-part
Wind Of The Spirit, Handt Hanson, *Worship And Praise*, p. 184
Pentecost Fire, Cool, CGA, Unison
Bless The Lord, O My Soul, Handel/Hopson, CGA, SAB

It would be special to have had the children make kites or windsocks or flags in red and white with doves or flames on them to decorate the church. Before the service starts, teach the congregation the word "peace" in several different languages. Explain that when you read the Acts passage during the scripture lessons, you would like each of them to choose one of those words to repeat several times after verse 4 of the reading. You will give them a sign for when this is to happen. Also ask them to make the sound of wind during verse 2 of the same passage.

Call to Worship (based on Psalm 104)
Leader: O God, how all encompassing are your works! Wisely you have made them all; the earth is full of your creatures.
People: Yonder is the sea, great and wide,
Children: So many creeping things you can't count them
Adults: Living things both large and small.
Leader: All creatures look to you to give them their food in due season.
Men: When you give to them, they gather it up.
Women: When you open your hand, they are filled with good things.
All: Giver of life, we praise you!

Prayer of Invocation
Breathe on us, breath of God, fill us and refresh us. We come to you on this Pentecost Sunday, ready to be filled with the Holy Spirit. We need to feel reinvigorated and refreshed. Open us to all we see, taste, smell, hear, and feel as we worship you. Amen.

Scripture Readings
Acts 2:1-21 and 1 Corinthians 12:3b-13 are two wonderful passages. Use the choral speaking choir with help from the congregation. This is truly a wonderful day for making a joyful noise. Have each member of the choir dress differently — use children if you can. They may have props, also; i.e. — a car mechanic in overalls, a woman in African dress, a child with a soccer ball and uniform, a businessman with a briefcase, a teenager with a guitar, a cook with chef's hat — are some suggestions. Have them come up out of the congregation.

Acts 2:1-21: *Have the speaking choir begin grouped close together.*

All: When the day of Pentecost had come, they were all together in one place. And suddenly from heaven there came a sound like the rush of a violent wind, and it filled the entire house where they were sitting.

(When they say, "Suddenly," have the congregation make wind sounds, and choir starts moving as if being blown. Move away from each other and into these positions):

```
        X X X X X
         X X X X
        X  P  X (P is for Peter)
```

Solo 1: Divided tongues, as of fire, appeared among them, and a tongue rested on each of them.

All: All of them were filled with the Holy Spirit and began to speak in other languages, as the Spirit gave them ability.

(The congregation will now speak their words for peace, repeatedly, six to eight times)

Solo 2: Now there were devout Jews from every nation under heaven living in Jerusalem. And at this sound the crowd gathered and was bewildered, because each one heard them speaking in the native language of them. Amazed and astonished, they asked,

3 Voices: "Are not all those who are speaking Galileans? And how is it that we hear, each of us, in our own native language? Parthians, Medes, Elamites, and residents of Mesopotamia, Judea and Cappadocia, Pontus and Asia, Phrygia and Pamphylia, Egypt, and the parts of Libya belonging to Cyrene, and visitors from Rome, both Jews and proselytes. Cretans and Arabs — in our own languages we hear them speaking about God's seeds of power."

All: All were amazed and perplexed, saying to one another, "What does this mean?"

2 Voices From The Back Row: But others sneered and said, "They are filled with new wine."

All: But Peter, standing with the eleven, raised his voice and addressed them,

Peter: *(Steps forward a step)* Men of Judea and all who live in Jerusalem, let this be known to you, and listen to what I say. Indeed, these are not drunk, as you suppose, for it is only 9 o'clock in the morning. No, this is what was spoken through the prophet Joel: "In the last days it will be, God declares, that I will pour out my Spirit upon all flesh, and your sons and your daughters shall prophesy. And I will show portents in the heaven above and signs on the earth below, blood, and fire, and smoky mist. The sun shall be turned to darkness and the moon to blood, before the coming of the Lord's great and glorious day. Then everyone who calls on the name of the Lord will be saved."

1 Corinthians 12:3b-13: *Have the choir move into one single line across the front of the church. Different soloists will say certain lines. When it is their verse, that person will step forward one step and raise or point out their prop or costume, to show their differences. They do not have to match the verse they are saying — it's just the differences that are important.*

All: And no one can say, "Jesus is Lord," except by the Holy Spirit.

Solo 1: Now there are varieties of gifts, but the same Spirit;

Solo 2: And there are varieties of services, but the same Lord;

Solo 3: And there are varieties of activities, but it is the same God who activates all of them in everyone.

All: To each is given the manifestation of the Spirit for the common good.

Solo 4: To one is given through the Spirit the utterance of wisdom,

Solo 5: And to another the utterance of knowledge according to the same Spirit,

Solo 6: To another faith by the same Spirit,

Solo 7: To another gifts of the healing by the one Spirit,

Solo 8: To another the working of miracles,

Solo 9: To another prophecy,

Solo 10: To another the discernment of spirits,

Solo 11: To another various kinds of tongues,

Solo 12: To another the interpretation of tongues.

Soloists 1-6: All these are activated by one and the same Spirit, who allots to each one individually just as the Spirit chooses.

Soloists 7-12: For just as the body is one and has many members, and all the members of the body, through many, are one body, so it is with Christ.

All: For in the one Spirit we were all baptized into one body — Jews or Greeks, slaves or free — and we were all made to drink of one Spirit.

Benediction (based on Psalm 104)
Leader: May the glory of God endure forever, may Yahweh rejoice in all works.
People: *(May be sung)* Spirit of the Living God, fall afresh on me,
Leader: God looks on the earth and it trembles, God touches the mountains and they smoke.
People: Spirit of the living God, fall afresh on me.
Leader: I will sing to Yahweh as long as I live: I will sing praise to my God while I have being.
People: Meld me, mold me,
Leader: May my meditation be pleasing to God, for I rejoice in my God.
People: Fill me, use me.
Leader: Bless the Lord, O my soul. Praise God!
People: Spirit of the living God, fall afresh on me.

The Holy Trinity

Genesis 1:1—2:4a **Psalm 8:1-9**
2 Corinthians 13:11-13 **Matthew 28:16-20**

Hymns
Sois la Semilla (You Are The Seed) (NCH528, MH583)
Lord, You Give The Great Commission (MH584, PH429)
We Shall Overcome (NCH570, MH533)
God, Who Stretched (CBH414, MH150, PH268)
Lord, Our Lord, Your Glorious Name (CBH157, PH163)
All Creatures Of Our God And King (LBW527, NCH17, PH455, MH62, CBH48)
All Things Bright And Beautiful (CBH156, MH147, PH267)
Wind Who Makes All The Winds Blow (NCH271, PH131, MH538)
I Sing The Mighty Power Of God (CBH46, MH152, PH288)
Of The Father's Love Begotten (CBH104, MH184, PH309)

Anthems
Lo, I Am With You, Daniel Moe, Augsburg, SATB
Genesis, William Payn, Flammer, 3 to 5-octave handbells
Great Is Your Name, John Chisom, Maranatha, *Songbook 10*, p. 828
Spirit, Wind Upon the Waters, Reeves, CGA, Unison/2-part
For Love Shall Be Our Song, Wagner, Unison

Call to Worship (based on Psalm 8)
Leader: Yahweh, how majestic is your name in all the earth! You have set your glory above the heavens,
People: When we look at your heavens, the work of your fingers, the moon and the stars that you have established;
Leader: What are we that you are mindful of us, that you care for us?
People: Yet you have made us a little lower than yourself, and crowned us with glory and honor.
All: Yahweh, how majestic is your name in all the earth!

Call to Confession
On Trinity Sunday we come to God in all aspects. We call on our Creator, remembering all that has been given to us. We honor our Redeemer, grateful for all that was given for us; and we are called by our Sustainer, who energizes us to continue the search. Let us confess our sins to our God, three in one.

Prayer of Confession
Gracious and kind God, we confess our confusion. It is so hard to think of you in all your wonder. We know you can do anything, but so often it doesn't seem like that. We are wrapped up in our own lives and our own desires, and so often we can't understand your vision for us and for all of your creation. We go against your vision when we destroy your creation and cause death and destruction to creatures and the natural world. We often reject your gift of new life in Christ by simply refusing to ask for forgiveness when we know we need it. We don't take

advantage of life-giving activity, preferring instead to stay safely at home, watching television, eating to excess, and thinking only of ourselves. Forgive us, God. Energize us to help others and to protect your creation. Open our hearts to all you have given us. Make us appreciative of all your gifts. Amen.

Assurance of Forgiveness
Jesus said, "All authority in heaven and on earth has been given to me. Remember, I am with you always, to the end of the age." Alleluia! Our sins have been forgiven. Amen.

Scripture Readings
Genesis 1:1—2:4a: *We rarely have the opportunity to hear the creation story. What better day to have the reenactment of God in all God's majesty? I would suggest one of two very different ways to present the creation story.*

1. If your congregation has a modern dancer or access to a dancer, she/he could interpret the story. Use a narrator at the pulpit and the voice of God outside of the sanctuary with a microphone. God could also be in the balcony — just so the person portraying God cannot be easily seen. The narrator should be able to read this poetry with great expression. The dancer would portray the drama of these words — moving around the sanctuary to a different place as each day is presented. Have the dancer interpret the seventh day right in the middle of the sanctuary.

2. Narration with art. This can be done several ways. Have seven banners made that depict what happens each day of the creation story. This could be an art project with your entire Sunday school, led by adult artists in your church. These banners should be simple, portraying only what is said.
>   Day 1 — dark, light, wind
>   Day 2 — dome (sky), waters above and below
>   Day 3 — land, seas, plants, trees, fruit, seed
>   Day 4 — light in sky: sun, moon, stars
>   Day 5 — water creatures, sky creatures
>   Day 6 — earth creatures, including humans
>   Day 7 — blessing and hallowing the creation; rest

These banners might be hung at the front of the sanctuary or over the heads of the congregation, or they could be created as cloth stained glass windows. Then simply read the story dramatically with God again not being seen.

Matthew 28:16-20: *This is a very short, simple passage, but Jesus' words are incredibly important. They need to be read well, by someone in authority. It could be pantomimed by one of the children's classes, and read by one of your more dramatic readers.*

Benediction (based on 2 Corinthians 13)
Leader: Brothers and Sisters, farewell. Paul in his letter to the Corinthians asks that we agree with each other, live in peace; and that the God of love and peace will be with you. Greet each other with the peace of God; know that all the saints also greet you. The grace of the Lord Jesus Christ, the love of God, and the communion of the Holy Spirit be with all of you. Amen.

Proper 4
Ordinary Time 9
Pentecost 2

Genesis 6:19-22; 7:24; 8:14-19 **Psalm 46**
Romans 1:16-17; 3:22b-28 (29-31) **Matthew 7:21-29**

Hymns
My Hope Is Built On Nothing Less (UM368, PH379, NCH403, CBH343)
A Mighty Fortress Is Our God (NCH439, CBH164, UM110, PH260)
Joys Are Flowing Like A River (NCH284, CBH301)
Glorious Things Of Thee Are Spoken (CBH619, UM731, PH446)
Holy, Holy, Holy (CHB120, UM614, PH138)
Lord, Dismiss Us With Your Blessing (NCH77, UM671, PH538)
We Would Be Building (NCH607)
The Word Of God Is Solid Ground (CBH 314)

Anthems
God Is Our Strength And Refuge, Philip Landgrove, Hope, Unison
Built On A Rock, J. Drummond Wolfe, Concordia, SATB
The Solid Rock, Tammy Waldrop, Lorenz, 3 to 5-octave handbells
A Living Faith, John Shepherd, Unison/2-part
Songs from *The Technicolor Promise,* Alan Pote, CGA, Unison/2-part

Call to Worship
Leader: Our hope is built on nothing less than Jesus' love and righteousness.
People: We dare not trust our earthly frame, but wholly lean on Jesus' name.
Leader: On Christ, the solid Rock, we stand;
People: All other ground is sinking sand.
All: All other ground is sinking sand.

Prayer of Invocation
Builder God, we come today to listen to the stories of faith. You are our refuge and our strength. This house of worship makes us feel safe and cared for — and brings us closer to you. Come to us in this place. Teach us how to build up this world we live in. Help us to build on solid ground, using strong materials, obeying your instructions, listening as you guide us while we work. Be with us on our journey. Amen.

Scripture Readings
Genesis 6:19-22; 7:24; 8:14-19: *Use this passage (Noah) for the Children's Sermon to use the "building" idea with and through God.*

Psalm 46: *This passage can be done well having the congregation read it as a litany. Have one side of the congregation read the uneven verses and the other side read the even verses. Have both sides say, "Selah," whenever it occurs.*

Matthew 7:21-29: *Have one person be Jesus teaching the folk in the synagogue. It would be best for them to have the passage memorized. After Jesus has finished verse 27, have him stop and simply "freeze" in place, and have another person come out and say verses 28 and 29 as though he is simply explaining what is going on (like an "overvoice" in a movie).*

Prayer of Dedication
God, we know that you are a God of all people. There is no distinction in your mind because of race, size, language, or gender. We bring our gifts to you today to be given to help all people. We ask that they assist the poor, the homeless, the hopeless in some way. Take our gifts and use them in your service. Amen.

Benediction
Leader: Jesus taught as one who had authority. He knew what he was saying.
People: Help us to listen and to believe. Then help us to tell others as if we have authority.
Leader: Go as people of God. Tell the story as if your life depends upon it.
People: Jesus, you are our model of ministry. Our life does depend on you. Amen.

Proper 5
Ordinary Time 10
Pentecost 3

Genesis 12:1-9 **Psalm 33:1-12**
Romans 4:13-25 **Matthew 9:9-13, 18-26**

Hymns
My Hope Is Built On Nothing Less (UM368, PH379, NCH403, CBH343)
The God Of Abraham Praise (NCH24, PH488)
For The Beauty Of The Earth (CBH89, UM92, PH473)
Softly And Tenderly Jesus Is Calling (CBH491, UM348)
Heal Us, Emmanuel, Hear Our Prayer (UM266)
This Is A Story Full Of Love (CHB315)
When In Our Music God Is Glorified (PH264)
Come Thou Fount Of Every Blessing (LBW499, NCH459, PH356)

Anthems
God Of The Promise, Richard Hillart, Augsburg, SATB
Rock-A-My-Soul, Ruth Artman, Hall Leonard, Mixed/2-part
Join Hands And Sing, J. D. Miller, Unison/2-part
Sing Alleluia, Sue Ellen Page, CGA, Unison

Call to Worship
Leader: Rejoice in our God. Praise befits the upright.
People: Praise our God with the lyre; make melody with the harp of ten strings.
Leader: Sing to Yahweh a new song; play skillfully on the strings, with loud shouts.
People: For the word of Yahweh is upright, and all God's work is done in faithfulness.
All: The earth is full of the steadfast love of our God.

Call to Confession
When Jesus heard that the Pharisees had asked, "Why does your teacher eat with tax collectors and sinners?" he said, "Those who are well have no need of a physician, but those who are sick do. Go and learn what this means, 'I desire mercy, not sacrifice.' I have come to call not the righteous but sinners." Let us come before God with our sins as we pray together the Prayer of Confession.

Prayer of Confession
Gracious and loving God, we think of ourselves as righteous and faithful people, but we are often led astray. We come to church each Sunday, but as the week goes on, we forget about our covenant with you. We get tired and irritable — we begin snapping at those we love most. We misuse the power that you have given us. We don't treat each other as we would like to be treated. Forgive us, O God. We do not model Jesus' behavior as he dines with outcasts and sinners. We would rather not have anything to do with people who aren't like us, or who don't behave the way we think they should behave. Forgive us, O God. Give us the humility to treat all people well. Remind us of our relationship with you. Keep us faithful. Amen.

Assurance of Pardon
A woman who had been suffering for twelve years came up behind Jesus and touched the fringes of his cloak, saying to herself, "If I only touch his cloak, I will be made well." Jesus turned to her and said, "Take heart, daughter, your faith has made you well." Take heart, O people. Have faith in Jesus, who died for our sins. We are made well. Amen.

Scripture Readings
Genesis 12:1-9: *This passage can easily be acted out by one of the children's Sunday school classes. It is mainly a conversation between God and Abram, but other people are involved. The Cast includes: Narrator, God, Abram, Lot, Sarai, and their servants. Lot and Sarai have no lines, and the rest of the class can be servants. God will be stationed near the altar. Abram and family can be sitting on the steps. When God speaks, all action ceases and Abram turns toward God. As the family travels, have them move around the sanctuary. Have the pulpit be the "oak of Moreh," where God again speaks to Abram and where Abram builds an altar. Then more movement to the middle of the sanctuary where they build another altar and pitch a tent (these movements can all be pantomimed). Then have the group travel on and out a sanctuary door.*

Matthew 9:9-13, 18-26: *A choral speaking choir could easily speak this passage. Speakers include (X) Choral Speakers, (L) Leader of Synagogue, (J) Jesus, (W) Woman with hemorrhage, and (P) Pharisee. Have the choir stand as follows:*

<pre>
          X X X X X
           L J W P P
</pre>

Voices 1 and 2: As Jesus was walking along, he saw a man called Matthew sitting at the tax booth; and he said to him,

Jesus: Follow me.

Voice 3: And he got up and followed him.

Voice 4: And as he sat at dinner in the house,

Voices 4, 5, and 6: Many tax collectors and sinners came and were sitting with him and his disciples.

Voice 1: When the Pharisees saw this, they said to his disciples,

Pharisees: Why does your teacher eat with tax collectors and sinners?

Voice 2: But when he heard this, he said,

Jesus: Those who are well have no need of a physician, but those who are sick. Go and learn what this means, "I desire mercy, not sacrifice." For I have come to call not the righteous but sinners.

Voices 3 and 4: While he was saying these things to them, suddenly a leader of the synagogue came in and knelt before him, saying,

Leader: My daughter has just died; but come and lay your hand on her and she will live.

All Voices: And Jesus got up and followed him, with his disciples.

Voice 5: Then suddenly a woman who had been suffering from hemorrhages for twelve years came up behind him and touched the fringe of his cloak, for she said to herself,

Woman: If I only touch his cloak, I will be made well.

Voice 6: Jesus turned, and seeing her he said,

Jesus: Take heart, daughter; your faith has made you well.

All Voices: And instantly the woman was made well.

Voice 1: When Jesus came to the leader's house and saw the flute players and the crowd making a commotion, he said,

Jesus: Go away, for the girl is not dead but sleeping.

Voices 2, 3, and 4: And they laughed at him.

Voices 5 and 6: But when the crowd had been put outside, he went in and took her by the hand, and the girl got up.

All Voices: And the report of this spread throughout the district.

Benediction
Leader: Abraham had faith that God would make him the father of many nations.
People: *(May be sung)* Faith of our fathers (the martyrs) living still, in spite of dungeon, fire, and sword,
Leader: A leader of the synagogue had faith that Jesus could give life to his daughter.
People: O how our hearts beat high with joy, when we recall their faith's reward.
Leader: A woman in the crowd believed that touching Jesus could heal her. Go out in faith and believe the good news!
All: Faith of our fathers (the martyrs), living faith! We would be true in life and death!

Proper 6
Ordinary Time 11
Pentecost 4

Genesis 18:1-15 (21:1-7)   Psalm 116:1-2, 12-19
Romans 5:1-8   Matthew 9:35—10:8 (9-23)

Hymns
We Are Dancing Sarah's Circle (NCH501)
I Love The Lord, Who Heard My Cry (NCH511, PH362)
More Love To Thee, O Christ (PH359)
What Wondrous Love Is This (CBH530, UM292, PH85)
Lift High The Cross (LBW377, NCH198, PH371, CBH321, UM159)
Ah, Holy Jesus (CBH254, PH93)
Lord, Whose Love In Humble Service (CBH369, UM581, PH427)
Come, Labor On (NCH532, PH415)

Anthems
Plenty Good Room, John Horman, Sommerset, SSA
Benedictus, David McK. Williams, H. W. Gray, Unison
Oh, What Beauty, Lord, Appears, Mozart/McKay, CGA, SATB
Now Join We To Praise The Creator, Michael Bedford

Call to Worship (based on Psalm 116)
Leader: I love my God, because God has heard my voice and my supplications.
People: Because God's ear has been inclined toward me, I will call on God as long as I live.
Leader: I will offer a thanksgiving sacrifice and call on Yahweh.
People: In the courts of the house of Yahweh, I will praise God forever!

Call to Confession
Abram's wife Sarai, laughed because she didn't believe that God would give her children when she was old. How often we laugh in the face of God's gifts. "It can't be true," we say, or "Not me!" Let us now confess our sins before God, first silently, then corporately. Let us pray.

Prayer of Confession
Faithful God, in the book of Romans we read the passage, "Suffering produces endurance, and endurance produces character, and character produces hope, and hope does not disappoint us, because God's love has been poured into our hearts through the Holy Spirit." Suffering is often when we grow in faith the most. It's the time when we recognize our need for you. But even then, when we pray to you, we hedge our bets. We make deals with you that we don't keep once the suffering has passed. How disappointed you must be in us, O God. Forgive us for our weakness in times of suffering and in times of great joy. Help us endure, increase our character, give us hope. We can't do it without you, God. Amen.

Assurance of Forgiveness
Romans 5 tells us that since we are justified by faith, we have peace with God through our Lord Jesus Christ through whom we have obtained access to this grace in which we stand. God proves his love for us in that while we still were sinners Christ died for us. Alleluia! We are forgiven. Amen.

Scripture Readings
Genesis 18:1-5: *The Genesis story is a wonderful story to use as drama. The cast includes: Narrator, Abraham, three Visitors, Sarah, Servant, Midwife, Baby. Try giving the passage to the junior or senior high Sunday school class and ask them to act it out for church. Give it to them four weeks ahead so that they can memorize the lines and use props. It is a great story for them to work through.*

Matthew 9:35—10:8 (9-23): *The Matthew passage is very long, but I think the instructions to the disciples are what are important. I would begin with 10:5 and continue through verse 23. The sermon can be what God's faithful people were asked to do — in that time of history. What are we being asked to do today? One person can read the passage.*

Call to Offering
What shall we return to God for all bounty given to us? The Psalmist answers, "I will lift up the cup of salvation and call on the name of God. I will pay my vows to Yahweh in the presence of all people." The ushers will now wait upon us for the morning offering.

Prayer of Dedication
Jesus said, "The harvest is plentiful but the laborers are few." Today we bring our harvest to you. We also bring ourselves as your laborers. Give us good work to do in your name, God. May our gifts of money go to feed the homeless and may our gifts of time be that of the hands that prepare the food. Help us to be peacemakers in the world today. Amen.

Benediction
Leader: As you go, proclaim the good news, "The kingdom of God has come near."
People: We will go out with joy and gratitude.
Leader: Remember the work of the twelve disciples. Go and seek the lost sheep. Give of yourselves freely.
People: We will go out with praise and thanksgiving.
Leader: It is not you who speak, but the Spirit of God speaking through you.
People: Fill us; use us — Spirit of the living God, fall afresh on us.

Proper 7
Ordinary Time 12
Pentecost 5

Genesis 21:8-21   **Psalm 86:1-10, 16-17**
Romans 6:1b-11   **Matthew 10:24-39**

Hymns
Great Is Thy Faithfulness (NCH423, PH276, UM140)
O Lord, Hear My Prayer (CBH348, Taize)
Lift High The Cross (NCH198, CBH321, UM159, PH371)
Crown Him With Many Crowns (CBH 116, UM327)
The Strife Is O'er (CBH263, UM306)
We Know That Christ Is Raised (UM610, PH495)
Take Up Your Cross (CBH536, PH393, UM415)
God's Eye Is On The Sparrow (NCH475)

Anthems
Great Is Thy Faithfulness, Cynthia Dobrinski, Agape, 3 to 5-octave handbells
O Savior Of The World, John Goss, G. Schirmer, SATB
It Is Well With My Soul, John Ness Beck, Beckenhorst, SATB
Lord Jesus, Be My Song, Kosche, CGA, Unison

Call to Worship (based on Psalm 86)
Leader: Give ear, O God, to our prayers; listen to our cries of supplication.
People: There is none like you, O God, and there are no works like yours.
Leader: All the nations you have made shall come and bow down before you, O God, and shall glorify your name.
People: For you are great and do wondrous things; you alone are God.

Call to Confession
God is always listening, even when we don't really want to talk. God knows our every thought. Let us come together to confess our sins to our God, even though we don't want to be reminded, or especially because we don't believe we have sinned. Let us pray.

Prayer of Confession
Give ear, O God, to our prayers. We ask that you hear our confession simply because it is so hard for us to confess. Every day we do something that strains our relationship with you. We listen to gossip, we yell at those we love the most, we lie about something we've done, and we let a homeless person pass by without helping. Every day we do something, Lord. We are so sorry, God, because we know we shouldn't. Some days, we try to excuse our behavior — and sometimes we just about convince ourselves — but not really. Forgive us, God, for our inhumanity. Amen.

Assurance of Forgiveness
Hear the good news as found in Romans 6. We know that Christ, being raised from the dead, will never die again; death no longer has dominion over him. The death he died, he died to sin, once for all; but the life he lives, he lives in God. So you also must consider yourselves dead to sin and alive to God in Christ Jesus. Alleluia! We are forgiven.

Scripture Readings
Genesis 21:8-21: *This passage is a hard one — casting out someone we care about. Have the choral speaking choir do this passage using three solo voices: Sarah, Hagar, and God.*

```
        X
       X X
      X H X
     S X X G
```

Voice 1: The child grew, and was weaned;

Voices 2, 3, and 4: And Abraham made a great feast on the day that Isaac was weaned.

Voice 5 (female): But Sarah saw the son of Hagar the Egyptian, whom she had borne to Abraham, playing with her son Isaac.

All: So she said to Abraham:

Sarah: Cast out this slave woman with her son; for the son of this slave woman shall not inherit along with my son Isaac.

Voices 6 and 7: The matter was very distressing to Abraham on account of his son.

Voice 1: But God said to Abraham,

God: Do not be distressed because of the boy and because of your slave woman; whatever Sarah says to you, do as she tells you, for it is through Isaac that offspring shall be named for you. As for the son of the slave woman, I will make a nation of him also, because he is your offspring.

Voices 2 and 3: So Abraham rose early in the morning, and took bread and a skin of water, and gave it to Hagar, putting it on her shoulder, along with the child, and sent her away.

Voice 3: And she departed, and wandered about in the wilderness of Beersheba. When the water in the skin was gone, she cast the child under one of the bushes.

Voice 5: Then she went and sat down opposite him a good way off, about the distance of a bowshot; for she said,

Hagar: Do not let me look on the death of the child.

Voice 5: And as she sat opposite him, she lifted up her voice and wept.

Voice 4: And God heard the voice of the boy; and the angel of God called to Hagar from heaven, and said to her,

God: What troubles you, Hagar? Do not be afraid; for God has heard the voice of the boy where he is. Come, lift up the boy and hold him fast with your hand, for I will make a great nation of him.

Voice 5: Then God opened her eyes and she saw a well of water. She went, and filled the skin with water, and gave the boy a drink.

All: God was with the boy, and he grew up;

Voice 6: He lived in the wilderness, and became an expert with the bow.

Voice 7: He lived in the wilderness of Paran; and his mother got a wife for him from the land of Egypt.

Matthew 10:24-39: *This passage continues Jesus' instructions to the disciples. Have the speaking choir stand in a straight line across the chancel.*

All: A disciple is not above the teacher, nor a slave above the master;

Voice 1: It is enough for the disciple to be like the teacher, and the slave like the master. If they have called the master of the house Beelzebub, how much more will they malign those of his household!

Voice 2: So have no fear of them; for nothing is covered up that will not be uncovered, and nothing secret that will not become known.

Voice 3: What I say to you in the dark, tell in the light; and what you hear whispered, proclaim from the housetops.

Voice 4: Do not fear those who kill the body but cannot kill the soul; rather fear him who can destroy both soul and body in hell.

Voice 5: Are not two sparrows sold for a penny? Yet not one of them will fall to the ground apart from your Father. And even the hairs of your head are all counted. So do not be afraid; you are of more value than many sparrows.

All: Everyone therefore who acknowledges me before others, I also will acknowledge before my Father in heaven; but whoever denies me before others, I also will deny before my Father in heaven.

Voice 6: Do not think that I have come to bring peace to the earth; I have not come to bring peace, but a sword.

Voices 7 and 8: For I have come to set a man against his father, and a daughter against her mother, and a daughter-in-law against her mother-in-law; and one's foes will be members of one's own household.

Voices 9 and 10: Whoever loves father or mother more than me is not worthy of me; and whoever loves son or daughter more than me is not worthy of me; and whoever does not take up the cross and follow me is not worthy of me.

All: Those who find their life will lose it, and those who lose their life for my sake will find it.

Benediction
Jesus said, "What I say to you in the dark, tell in the light; and what you hear whispered, proclaim from the housetops." Arise, your light has come, the Spirit's call obey. With energy and love, go from this place with courage and fortitude. Let us obey Christ's call to newness of life in all we do and say. And may the peace of God go with us. Amen.

Proper 8
Ordinary Time 13
Pentecost 6

Genesis 22:1-14   **Psalm 13**
Romans 6:12-23   **Matthew 10:40-42**

Hymns
Faith Of Our Fathers (the Martyrs) (LBW500, NCH381, CBH413, UM710)
Amazing Grace (NCH547, CBH143, UM378, PH280)
Take My Life (CBH389, UM399, PH341)
Eternal Light (CBH518, PH340)
Every Time I Feel The Spirit (UM404, PH315)
Blessed Assurance (PH341, UM369)
Where Cross The Crowded Ways Of Life (NCH543, CBH405, PH408)
There's A Spirit In The Air (PH433)

Anthems
God Will Provide A Lamb, Michael Card, *The Beginning,* Solo
Amazing Grace, George Linn, Abingdon, SATB
Rock-A-My Soul, Hopson, CGA, Unison 2-part
Sing Thankful Songs (Cantad Cancion de Gratitud), Arr. Gay, Unison 2-part

Call to Worship
Leader: Jesus said, "Whoever welcomes you welcomes me, and whoever welcomes me welcomes the one who sent me."
People: We welcome all who wish to offer praise to the living God.
Leader: All who come to this house of God receive welcome and nurture.
People: Let us worship our God with shouts of praise!
All: Alleluia! Amen.

Call to Confession
"How long, O Lord? How long must I bear pain in my soul?" says the Psalmist. But we know God is with us to listen and forgive. Let us confess together those things for which we beg forgiveness.

Prayer of Confession
God, what is it that you ask of us? We don't always know. In fact, we rarely know. Is it because what you ask of us is too hard, and we just don't want to listen? Or is it because it is too easy, and we can't believe it can be that easy? Forgive us, God, for not discerning your will for us. We struggle through our daily existence, trying to do what is right and good and pleasing in your sight. But we are constantly confounded by noise and information that clutters our mind — and our connection with you. Help us, God, to make time in our day simply to be quiet and listen for and with you. Forgive us for succumbing to the craziness of the culture. Hear our prayer, O God.

Assurance of Forgiveness
Have you heard the good news? Jesus died for us so that we could be saved from our sins. In one incredible act, we are forgiven. Praise the Lord for such a great gift!

Scripture Readings
Genesis 22:1-14: *This passage is perfect for drama. It could be done by children, youth, or adults. It is interesting that there is no emotion mentioned in the scripture passage at all, but it is hard to imagine that there wouldn't be incredible stress, worry, and fear in Abraham, and Sarah who has been left at home, and even Isaac as they got closer to the act itself. Depending on the thrust of the sermon, the story could be done using all the emotions — or could simply be a literal interpretation of the story. Cast includes: Narrator (speaking from the lectern or pulpit), God (a voice offstage), Abraham, two young men who are helpers, and Isaac. Have Abraham start at left front. After God speaks to him, he would go to the middle of the center aisle to prepare for the trip. The group would then wander slowly up the center aisle. The altar could be the place where the fire is built and Isaac is to be sacrificed. A stuffed sheep could be used in the floral decorations for the day so that Abraham could find it to sacrifice instead of Isaac. The donkey is a dilemma so in the script, the young men carry wood and matches to give to Isaac.*

Narrator: God tested Abraham.

God: Abraham!

Abraham: Here I am.

God: Take your son, your only son Isaac, whom you love, and go to the land of Moriah; and offer him there as a burnt offering on one of the mountains that I shall show you. *(Abraham looks completely stricken, but slowly walks to center aisle)*

Narrator: So Abraham rose early the next morning, took two of his young men and his son Isaac, cut the wood for the burnt offering *(Each person takes two or three sticks/logs)*, and set out and went to the place in the distance that God had shown him. *(Begin moving around the sanctuary. End up at the bottom of the steps to the chancel)* On the third day, Abraham looked up and saw the place far away.

Abraham: *(To young men)* Stay here and make camp; the boy and I will go over there; we will worship, and then we will come back to you.

Narrator: Abraham took the wood of the burnt offering and laid it on his son Isaac, and he himself carried the fire and the knife. *(Abraham also needs to have rope)* So the two of them walked on together.

Isaac: Father?

Abraham: Yes, my son.

Isaac: The fire and the wood are here, but where is the lamb for a burnt offering?

Abraham: *(With sorrow)* God will provide the lamb for a burnt offering, my son. *(Isaac looks up at him)*

Narrator: When they came to the place that God had shown him, Abraham built an altar there and laid the wood in order. He bound his son Isaac *(Abraham ties Isaac with the rope)*, and laid him on the altar, on top of the wood. *(Abraham builds fire on ground in front of altar. Isaac sits in front of the wood, looking very frightened, but not saying anything)* Then Abraham reached out his hand and took the knife to kill his son.

God: Abraham, Abraham!

Abraham: *(Lowering the knife)* Here I am.

God: Do not lay your hand on the boy or do anything to him; for now I know that you fear God, since you have not withheld your son, your only son, from me.

Narrator: *(Abraham unties Isaac and hugs him, then looks around)* And Abraham looked up and saw a ram, caught in a thicket by its horns. Abraham went and took the ram and offered it up as a burnt offering instead of his son. *(Abraham places sheep in the middle of the wood — then slowly walks back to young men and heads up the middle aisle and out)* So Abraham called that place, "Yahweh will provide"; as it is said to this day, "On the mount of Yahweh it shall be provided."

Matthew 10:40-42: *This passage can be read from the pulpit. It is the ending of Jesus' instructions to his disciples. The best way to connect these two passages may be through the image of obedience and reward.*

Benediction
Leader: Whoever gives even a cup of cold water in the name of a disciple — receives their reward.
People: We go, offering ourselves and our faith to those whom we meet.
All: Jesus Christ is our reward for every act of kindness.
Leader: Go, in the name of God our Creator, Christ our Redeemer, and with the Holy Spirit who will sustain you. Amen.

Proper 9
Ordinary Time 14
Pentecost 7

Genesis 24:34-38, 42-49, 58-67   Psalm 45:10-17 or Song of Solomon 2:8-13
Romans 7:15-25a   Matthew 11:16-19, 25-30

Hymns
Come, Thou Fount Of Every Blessing (LBW499, NCH459, PH356, CBH521, UM400)
Camina, Pueblo de Dios (Go Forth, O People Of God) (NCH614, UM305)
Make Me A Captive, Lord (CBH539, UM421, PH378)
How Clear Is Our Vocation, Lord (CBH54, PH419)
There Is A Place Of Quiet Rest (CBH5, UM472, PH527)
I Heard The Voice Of Jesus Say (NCH489, CBH493)
There Is A Balm In Gilead (NCH553, CBH627, UM375, PH394)
Just As I Am (CBH516, UM357, PH370)

Anthems
Come Unto Me, Dale Wood, AMSI, SATB
Be Thou My Vision, Alice Parker, Hinshaw, SATB
El-Shaddai, John Thompson, Word, 2-part mixed
Jesus, Son Of God Most High, Lindh and Cox, CGA, Unison, optional descant, flute, guitar, congregation

Call to Worship
Leader: In the heat of the summer, we come together to praise God!
People: It is good and pleasant to give God praise!
Leader: We remember God's goodness to all God's people.
People: We listen to the stories of God's grace and the people's struggle.
All: Let us worship God.

Prayer of Invocation
Covenanting God, we know we are part of your promise to Abraham and his descendants. You are a great God who promises to be faithful generation after generation. Help us to keep the faith and continue the struggle. As we listen to your story spoken through music and word, may we be renewed in our own faith. Give us energy to continue your work in this world. Through Jesus Christ we pray. Amen.

Scripture Readings
Genesis 24:34-38, 58-67: *The Genesis passage can be used as a chancel drama, but because of the number of people involved, it might be better done by a choral speaking choir. Voices needed include Abraham's Servant, Rebekah, Rebekah's Brothers, and the choir as Narrator.*

```
        X X X X
         B X X
          B R
          AS
```

Servant: I am Abraham's servant. The Lord has greatly blessed my master, and he has become wealthy; he has given him flocks and herds, silver and gold, male and female slaves, camels and donkeys. And Sarah, my master's wife, bore a son to my master when she was old; and he has given him all that he has. My master made me swear, saying, "You shall not take a wife for my son from the daughters of the Canaanites, in whose land I live; but you shall go to my father's house, to my kindred and get a wife for my son." I said to my master, "Perhaps the woman will not follow me."

I came today to the spring, and said, "O Lord, the God of my master Abraham, if now you will only make successful the way I am going! I am standing here by the spring of water; let the young woman who comes out to draw, to whom I shall say, 'Please give me a little water from your jar to drink,' and who will say to me, 'Drink, and I will draw for your camels also' — let her be the woman whom the Lord has appointed for my master's son." Before I had finished speaking in my heart, there was Rebekah coming out with her water jar on her shoulder; and she went down to the spring and drew. I said to her, "Please let me drink." She quickly let down her jar from her shoulder, and said,

Rebekah: Drink, and I will also water your camels.

Servant: So I drank, and she also watered the camels. Then I asked her, "Whose daughter are you?" She said,

Rebekah: The daughter of Bethuel, Nahor's son, whom Milcah bore to him.

Servant: *(To audience)* So I put the ring on her nose, and the bracelets on her arms. Then I bowed my head and worshiped the Lord, and blessed the Lord, the God of my master Abraham, who had led me by the right way to obtain the daughter of my master's kinsman for his son. "Now then, if you will deal loyally and truly with my master, tell me; and if not, tell me, so that I may turn either to the right hand or to the left."

Back Row: And they called Rebekah, and said to her,

Brothers: Will you go with this man?

Rebekah: I will.

Back Row: So they sent away their sister Rebekah and her nurse along with Abraham's servant and his men. And they blessed Rebekah and said to her,

Brothers: May you, oh, sister, become thousands of myriads; may your offspring gain possession of the gates of their foes.

1 Female Voice: Then Rebekah and her maids rose up, mounted the camels, and followed the man; thus the servant took Rebekah, and went his way.

1 Voice: Now Isaac had come from Beerlahiroi, and was settled in the Negeb. Isaac went out in the evening to walk in the field; and looking up, he saw camels coming. And Rebekah looked up, and when she saw Isaac, she slipped quickly from the camel, and said to the servant,

Rebekah: Who is the man over there, walking in the field to meet us?

Servant: It is my master.

1 Female Voice: Then she took her veil and covered herself.

1 Voice: And the servant told Isaac all the things that he had done.

Another Voice: Then Isaac brought her into his mother Sarah's tent. He took Rebekah, and she became his wife; and he loved her.

All: So Isaac was comforted after his mother's death.

Romans 7:15-25a: *This is a soliloquy by Paul as he struggles with his own sin. It would be best done if memorized, but could be read. The person should be moving around, as if arguing with himself and talking to God.*

Matthew 11:16-19, 25-30: *This is a soliloquy in which Jesus is teaching. It could be done in the same way as Paul, by the same person, but Jesus could be sitting or leaning. It is not as filled with passion as the Paul passage. When the speaker comes to verses 28-38, he should go into the congregation, as if Jesus was moving through the crowd.*

Call to Offering
Jesus said, "Come unto me all you that are weary and are carrying heavy burdens, and I will give you rest." Let us give freely of what we have been given to help others whose burdens are heavier than our own.

Prayer of Dedication (from the hymn *We Give Thee But Thine Own*)
Leader: We give you back your own, whatever the gift may be.
People: All that we have is yours alone, a trust, O God, from you.
Leader: To comfort and to bless, to find a balm for sadness,
People: To tend the lone and homeless is our own work for you.
Leader: And we believe your word, though dim our faith may be
People: Whatever we do for you, O God, we do it in your name. Amen.

Benediction
Leader: Jesus said, "Come unto me, all you that are weary."
People: We came and found refreshment for our souls.
Leader: Jesus said, "Take my yoke upon you, and learn from me."
People: We have learned from your word. We are eager to do your will, remembering that your yoke is easy and your burden light.
Leader: With joy in the name of Christ, you are blessed. Amen.

Proper 10
Ordinary Time 15
Pentecost 8

Genesis 25:19-34   Psalm 119:105-112
Romans 8:1-11   Matthew 13:1-9, 18-23

Hymns
Immortal, Invisible, God Only Wise (LBW526, NCH1, PH263, CBH70, UM103)
Spirit Of God, Descend Upon My Heart (LBW486, NCH290, PH326, CBH502, UM500)
O Word Of God Incarnate (NCH315, PH327)
O For A Closer Bond (Walk) With God (NCH450, PH396, 397)
We Plow The Fields And Scatter (LBW362, PH560, CBH96)
God Is Here Among Us (CBH16)
You Are Salt For The Earth (CBH226)
Almighty God, Your Word Is Cast (NCH318)

Anthems
Blessed Are They, Jennings, CGA, SATB
Thy Word Is A Lamp, Amy Grant/Michael Smith, *Lift Up Your Hearts,* p. 85.
The Word Of God, Jean Berger, Augsburg, SATB w/instruments
The Kingdom Of God, Bolt, 2-part, 2-part Mixed

Call to Worship
Leader: Blest be the tie that binds our lives with all the saints.
People: Praise God for Abraham and Sarah, for Isaac and Rebekah, and all the men and women who covenanted with their Creator.
Leader: We thank God for the greatest gift, his son Jesus Christ,
People: And for all his loyal followers: for Mary and Martha, Paul, Lydia, Peter, and the early Christians who lived with daily persecution.
Leader: We are here because of their faithfulness.
All: Let us worship God.

Call to Confession
Like the Psalmist, we come to God with our shortcomings, asking for God's care and forgiveness. We are severely afflicted, and we ask our God for life. Let us pray together.

Prayer of Confession
O merciful and just God, we come to you today full of guilt. We have so much trouble staying faithful to your law, and to Jesus' model of kindness and generosity. We leave the house and are immediately immersed in traffic that causes us to lose our temper. We treat those anonymous people so badly, God, because we know we'll never see them again. We go to work or to school and get caught up in gossip. We become fearful that we won't do a good job, and immediately think about cheating or taking the easy way out. We don't mean to, God. Each evening we think, "I have to change my way of treating others," but we continually repeat our behavior.

Forgive us, God. Walk with us. Whisper in our ear when we are tempted to treat someone with disdain. Open our ears that we might hear you and obey. Amen.

Assurance of Forgiveness
Paul told the believers in Rome, "There is therefore now no condemnation for those who are in Christ Jesus. For the law of the Spirit of life in Christ Jesus has set you free from the law of sin and of death. If Christ is in you, the spirit is life because of righteousness." Alleluia. You are forgiven. Amen.

Scripture Readings
Genesis 25:19-34: *A choral speaking choir may read the Genesis passage. Placement of the choir might look like this:*

```
           7    8
           5    6
           3    4
           1    2
         Esau  Jacob
```

All: These are the descendants of Isaac, Abraham's son:

Voice 1: Abraham was the father of Isaac

Voice 2: And Isaac was forty years old when he married Rebekah, daughter of Bethuel the Aramean of Paddanaram,

Voice 3: Sister of Laban the Aramean.

Voice 4: Isaac prayed to the Lord for his wife, because she was barren; and the Lord granted his prayer, and his wife Rebekah conceived.

Voice 5: The children struggled together within her; and she said, "If it is to be this way, why do I live?"

Voice 6: So she went to inquire of the Lord. And the Lord said to her,

Voice 7: Two nations are in your womb, and two peoples born of you shall be divided; the one shall be stronger than the other, the elder shall serve the younger.

Voice 8: When her time to give birth was at hand, there were twins in her womb. The first came out red, all his body like a hairy mantle; so they named him Esau.

Voice 7: Afterward his brother came out, with his hand gripping Esau's heel; so he was named Jacob.

Voice 1: Isaac was sixty years old when she bore them.

Voice 2: When the boys grew up, Esau was a skillful hunter, a man of the field,

Voice 3: While Jacob was a quiet man, living in tents.

Voice 4: Isaac loved Esau, because he was fond of game;

Voice 5: But Rebekah loved Jacob.

Voice 6: Once when Jacob was cooking a stew, Esau came in from the field, and he was famished.

Voice 8: Esau said to Jacob,

Esau: Let me eat some of that red stuff, for I am famished!

Voice 1: Therefore he was called Edom. Jacob said,

Jacob: First sell me your birthright.

Esau: I am about to die; of what use is a birthright to me?

Jacob: Swear to me first.

Voice 2: So he swore to him, and sold his birthright to Jacob.

Voice 3: Then Jacob gave Esau bread and lentil stew, and he ate and drank, and rose and went his way.

All: Thus Esau despised his birthright.

Matthew 18:1-9, 18-23: *This passage simply needs an introduction and then is a soliloquy by Jesus. It would be best done memorized, but could be read with much rehearsal. The person playing Jesus should treat it as if he were telling the story and then teaching the explanation that follows.*

Narrator: (*Jesus comes from stage right and walks up the steps to the chancel area as the Narrator reads*) At that time the disciples came to Jesus and asked, "Who is the greatest in the kingdom of heaven?" He called them, and said,

Jesus: Truly I tell you, unless you change and become like children, you will never enter the kingdom of heaven. Whoever becomes humble like this child is the greatest in the kingdom of heaven. Whoever welcomes one such child in my name welcomes me. If any of you put a stumbling block before one of these little ones who believe in me, it would be better for you if a great millstone were fastened around your neck and you were drowned in the depth of the sea. Woe to the world because of stumbling blocks! Occasions for stumbling are bound to come, but woe to the one by whom the stumbling block comes! If your hand or your foot causes you to stumble, cut it off and throw it away; it is better for you to enter life maimed or lame than to have two hands or two feet and to be thrown into the eternal fire. And if your eye causes you to stumble, tear it out and throw it away; it is better for you to enter life with one eye than to have two eyes and to be thrown into the hell of fire. Truly I tell you, whatever you bind on earth will be bound in heaven, and whatever you loose on earth will be loosed in heaven. Again, truly I tell you, if two of you agree on earth about anything you ask, it will be done for you by my Father in heaven. For where two or three are gathered in my name, I am there among them.

Narrator: Then Peter came and said to him, "Lord, if another member of the church sins against me, how often should I forgive? As many as seven times seven?" Jesus said to him,

Jesus: Not seven times, but, I tell you, seventy-seven times.

Call to Offering
As the ushers wait on us for the morning offering, remember the parable of the sower. Sow your seeds on good earth, where they can multiply and give life. God loves a cheerful giver.

Prayer of Dedication
We thank you, God, for the beautiful day, the sun that allows the seed to grow. We give you today what we hope is good seed. Take our offering and make use of it in ways that will only help people grow. This we ask in the name of Christ Jesus, the great storyteller and sower. Amen.

Benediction
Leader: Go forth with a new resolve to sow only good seed on healthy ground.
People: We will not go toward the thorns, only to be caught where the seed cannot grow.
Leader: God's word is a lamp to our feet and a light to our path. Do not wander off the path.
All: God is our light and our guide. Amen.

Proper 11
Ordinary Time 16
Pentecost 9

Genesis 28:10-19a **Psalm 139:1-12, 23-24**
Romans 8:12-25 **Matthew 13:24-30, 36-43**

Hymns
There Is A Wideness In God's Mercy (LBW290, NCH23, PH298, CBH145, UM121)
Nearer, My God, To Thee (NCH606, UM528)
Out Of The Depths (UM515, CBH133, NCH483)
Precious Lord, Take My Hand (PH404, UM474, CBH575, NCH472)
Prayer Is The Soul's Sincere Desire (CBH572, NCH508, UM492)
In The Bulb There Is A Flower (CBH614, NCH433, UM707)
If Thou But Trust In God To Guide Me (CBH576, NCH410, PH282, UM142)
Come, Ye Thankful People, Come (UM694, CBH94, NCH422, PH551)

Anthems
Every Time I Feel The Spirit, William Dawson, Tuskegee Music Press, SATB or TTBB
Jacob's Ladder, Kevin McChesney, Alfred Pub., 2 to 3-octave handbells
Psalm 139, Pote, CGA, SATB
We Are Children Of Our God, Michael Jothen, Unison/2-part

Call to Worship
Leader: Praise God for the heat of summer
People: God has created the seasons in all their intricacies
Leader: The heat of the sun fills our spirits and reminds us of all God's greatness.
People: As we come inside to get out of the heat, we come to worship all of God's creation.
Leader: Let us be filled with the heat of God's loving presence.
All: Surely our God is in this place! Amen.

Prayer of Invocation
All-encompassing God, we are in awe of you. We come to you in all of our seasons: when we are joy-filled or grief-filled, when our hearts are filled with love and when we're crippled with hatred, at the birth of a new baby, and at the death of a parent. You are the head of this family of faith, and we come to sit at the table and be fed. On this hot summer day, we are eager to hear your word and learn more of your desires for us. Teach us, O God, all that you want us to know. We are here to listen and be inspired to do your will. Amen.

Scripture Readings
Genesis 28:10-19a: *This passage would really be a good one to have older elementary students dramatize. The cast includes a Narrator, Jacob, Angels (four or more), and God. Props include several large rocks, eight to twelve inches in diameter, a step ladder, and a small container for "pretend" oil. Jacob wears a typical biblical costume. God and Angels can wear white. Angels could have halos/wings if preferred, but not so they get in the way of their ability to go up and down the ladder.*

Narrator: Jacob left Beer-Sheba and went toward Haran. *(Jacob comes from back of sanctuary and up steps to chancel. Large stones are piled in front of the altar. Jacob sets up camp and chooses a stone to be his pillow)* He came to a certain place and stayed there for the night, because the sun had set. Taking one of the stones of the place, he put it under his head and lay down in that place. *(Jacob lies down with a stone for his pillow)* And he dreamed that there was a ladder set up *(Four or more Angels carry a ladder out and set it in front of Jacob. They take turns climbing up about three steps on the ladder)* on the earth, the top of it reaching to heaven; and the angels of God were ascending and descending on it. And the Lord stood beside him and said,

God: *(Comes out stage right and stands right behind Jacob who is still asleep)* I am Yahweh, God of Abraham your father and the God of Isaac; the land on which you lie I will give to you and to your offspring; and your offspring shall be like the dust of the earth, and you shall spread abroad to the west and to the east and to the north and to the south; and all the families of the earth shall be blessed in you and in your offspring. Know that I am with you and will keep you wherever you go, and will bring you back to this land, for I will not leave you until I have done what I have promised you.

Narrator: Then Jacob woke from his sleep and said,

Jacob: *(Wakes up, stretches and stands up)* Surely Yahweh is in this place, and I did not know it!

Narrator: And he was afraid, and said,

Jacob: How awesome is this place! This is none other than the house of God, and this is the gate of heaven.

Narrator: So Jacob rose early in the morning, and he took the stone that he had put under his head *(Jacob piles rocks on top of each other and places a rock on the top. Then he pulls a flask from his pocket and pretends to pour oil over the rocks)* and set it up for a pillar and poured oil on the top of it.

Jacob: I will call this place Bethel.

Narrator: but the name of the city was Luz at the first.

Matthew 13:24-30, 36-43: *As a reader reads Matthew 13:24-30, a Sunday school class could pantomime the parable. The cast includes: the Householder, an Enemy, and Field Servants who discover the weeds. Beginning with verse 36, the children might become the disciples who ask what the parable means. They might sit at the reader's feet, and say, "Explain to us the parable of the weeds of the field." Then the reader may finish the passage as if teaching the disciples.*

Call to Offering
As we gather the offering today, may all that we give be used to sow the good seed of kindness in the world. The ushers will wait upon us for the morning offering.

Pastoral Prayer
O God, you have searched us and know us. The psalmist tells us that even before a word is on our tongues, you know what we are going to say. And yet we are compelled to pray together to thank you for all your good gifts to us. We thank you for the sun which makes the crops grow. We thank you for the cool of the evenings which produces the dew that keeps the earth cooler. You are a great God, and we love you. We ask today for your oversight of your world, God. So many of the people live in poverty, sickness, and war. Whisper into the ears of the world leaders, God. Encourage them to lust after peace and not power. Impel each of us to befriend someone different from ourselves — to understand that despite our differences we are very much alike.

God, we also ask your healing presence with all those who are sick, grieving, and filled with worry. Help those whom we name today to know that you are with them on their journey. Give them your steadfast love to walk through their lives without so much fear of the unknown. As the Psalmist says, "Hem us in, behind and before, and lay your hand upon us." Give us your peace. Amen.

Benediction
Leader: All who are led by the Spirit of God are children of God.
People: Lead us, Holy Spirit.
Leader: Go in hope, go in peace, go in love.
People: Lead us, Holy Spirit. Amen.

Proper 12
Ordinary Time 17
Pentecost 10

Genesis 29:15-28 **Psalm 105:1-11, 45b**
Romans 8:26-39 **Matthew 13:31-33, 44-52**

Hymns
Sing Praise To God (NCH6, UM126, PH483)
Guide Me, O Thou Great Jehovah (CBH582, NCH18, 19, UM127, PH281)
Like The Murmur Of The Dove's Song (NCH270, UM544, PH314)
O Love That Will Not Let Me Go (NCH485, UM480, PH342)
Jesus Priceless Treasure (CBH595, NCH480, UM532, PH365)
Thine Is The Glory (CBH269, NCH253, UM308, PH122)
By Gracious Powers (NCH412, UM517, PH342)
The Kingdom Of God (CBH224, UM275)

Anthems
The Love Of God, Natalie Sleeth, SATB
Seek The Lord, Anna Laura Page, Hinshaw, SATB
Sing God A Simple Song, Leonard Bernstein in *Ecumenical Praise*, Agape, Unison
We Will Sing For Joy, Scarlotti/Lowe, CGA, Unison

Call to Worship (based on Psalm 105)
Leader: O give thanks to Yahweh, call out the name, make known God's deeds among the peoples.
People: Sing to Yahweh, and tell of all God's wonderful works.
Leader: Glory in God's holy name; let the hearts of those who seek God rejoice.
People: Seek God's presence continually.
All: We come seeking Yahweh.

Call to Confession
The Spirit helps us in our weakness, says Paul; for we do not know how to pray as we ought, but that very Spirit intercedes with sighs too deep for words. Let us now pray together our Prayer of Confession.

Prayer of Confession
Searching God, in the book of Romans we are told that "all things work together for good for those who love God because we are called according to your purpose." But we don't act as though we believe that. We act as though we are the only one that has our interests at heart. Perhaps that's because we don't listen for your voice telling us who we are and whose we are. We want to control our lives and the outcome of our lives. We don't necessarily want what you have in mind for us. We covet wealth and material things, you ask us to love each other. We covet power; you tell us God loves the humble. Help us, God, to remember who gave us life. No one can separate us from the love of God through Jesus Christ, our Savior. We believe — help our unbelief. Amen.

Assurance of Forgiveness

Sisters and Brothers, remember the words of Paul: Neither death, nor life, nor angels, nor rulers, nor things present, nor things to come, nor powers, nor height, nor depth, nor anything else in all creation, will be able to separate us from the love of God in Christ Jesus our Lord. Alleluia! We are forgiven. Amen.

Scripture Readings

Genesis 29:15-28: *Use a choral speaking choir for this passage.*

```
            1       2       3
        4       5       6       7
              Leah        Rachel
                Laban   Jacob
```

Voice 5: Then Laban said to Jacob,

Laban: Because you are my kinsman, should you therefore serve me for nothing? Tell me, what shall your wages be?

Voice 1: Now Laban had two daughters,

Voice 4: The name of the elder was Leah

Voice 7: And the name of the younger was Rachel.

Leah: Leah's eyes were lovely,

Rachel: And Rachel was graceful and beautiful.

Voice 6: Jacob loved Rachel, so he said,

Jacob: I will serve you seven years for your younger daughter Rachel.

Laban: It is better that I give her to you than that I should give her to any other man; stay with me.

Voices 1, 2, and 3: So Jacob served seven years for Rachel, and they seemed to him but a few days because of the love he had for her.

Voice 5: Then Jacob said to Laban,

Jacob: Give me my wife that I may go in to her, for my time is completed.

All Voices: So Laban gathered together all the people of the place, and made a feast.

Leah: But in the evening he took his daughter Leah and brought her to Jacob; and he went in to her.

Voice 4: Laban gave his maid Zilpah to his daughter Leah to be her maid.

Voices 1, 2, and 3: When morning came, it was Leah!

Voice 7: And Jacob said to Laban,

Jacob: What is this you have done to me? Did I not serve with you for Rachel? Why then have you deceived me?

Laban: This is not done in our country — giving the younger before the firstborn. Complete the week of this one, and we will give you the other also in return for serving me another seven years.

Voice 6: Jacob did so, and completed her week;

All Voices: Then Laban gave him his daughter Rachel as a wife.

Matthew 13:31-33, 44-52: *Have someone dressed as Jesus for this passage. Put the different objects of the parables on the altar, or on a table in front of the sanctuary. Have them decoratively assembled in addition to flowers. These would include an attractive glass bottle with mustard seeds, a package of yeast, a loaf of bread, a small expensive-looking box, a necklace of pearls, and a fish net. As Jesus tells the different parables, he will use the objects as props, picking them up as he speaks. When he gets to verse 49, he will move closer to the congregation. When he asks, "Have you understood all this?" Jesus will speak directly to the congregation. If they don't respond, he will say, "Have you?" Then he will continue, "Therefore every scribe who has been trained for the kingdom of heaven is like the master of a household who brings out of his treasure what is new and what is old."*

Call to Offering
We know that all things work together for good for those who love God, who are called according to God's purpose. Let us come together to work for good by giving our morning offering generously.

Prayer of Dedication
God, we know that you love us. Not just those of us sitting here in these pews, but all of us. May this offering today go to help your people who need it the most: the lonely, the sick of heart and of body, the hungry, and the homeless. May our gifts help them to know that nothing can separate them from the love of Christ. Amen.

Benediction
Leader: The kingdom of heaven is like a mustard seed.
People: May we be like the tree, protecting God's creatures.
Leader: The kingdom of heaven is like a treasure hidden in a field.
People: May we continue to search until we find it.
Leader: The kingdom of heaven is like a fishing net.
People: May we be the fishermen, pulling up the nets.
Leader: Have you understood all of this?
People: Yes. We go in the name of our God. Amen.

Proper 13
Ordinary Time 18
Pentecost 11

Genesis 32:22-31 **Psalm 17:1-7, 15**
Romans 9:1-5 **Matthew 14:13-21**

Hymns
Break Now The Bread Of Life (NCH321, CBH360, UM599, PH329)
Come, O Thou Traveler Unknown (UM386, CBH503)
God Is Here (NCH70, PH461)
Holy Spirit, Truth Divine (LBW257, NCH63, PH321)
Our God, To Whom We Turn (NCH37, PH278)
Sweet Hour Of Prayer (NCH505)
Sheaves Of Summer/Una Espiga (NCH338, PH518)
You Satisfy The Hungry Heart (PH521)

Anthems
Asleep On Holy Ground, Michael Card, *The Beginning,* Solo
All My Hope On God Is Founded, Michael Burkhardt, MorningStar, SATB, Unison/congregation
Song For Beginnings, Riehle, CGA, Unison/2-part
Psalm 17, Marshall, Unison/2-part

Call to Worship (based on Psalm 17)
Leader: O God, attend to our cries ...
People: Give ear to our prayers.
Leader: My steps have held fast to your paths; my feet have not slipped.
People: I call upon you, for you will answer me, O God.
Leader: Incline your ear to us, hear our words.
All: Show your steadfast love, O savior of all who seek refuge. Amen.

Prayer of Invocation
O God of Abraham, Isaac, and Jacob, be with us today as we listen to your word spoken and interpreted. Open our ears that all we hear today — the Bible stories, the wonderful music — fills us with the desire to follow you in all of our actions. Be with us, God, and guide the way, in this and every coming day. Amen.

Scripture Readings
Genesis 32:22-31: *Use a choral speaking choir for this passage.*

```
                    X            X
         Side 1     X                  X     Side 2
                   X X              X X
                      Man and Jacob
```

Side 1: The same night he got up and took his two wives, his two maids, and his eleven children, and crossed the ford of the Jabbok.

Side 2: He took them and sent them across the stream, and likewise everything that he had.

Both Sides: Jacob was left alone; and a man wrestled with him until daybreak. *(Jacob and Man turn toward each other)*

Side 1: When the man saw that he did not prevail against Jacob, he struck him on the hip socket. *(Man brings hand down at Jacob's waist)*

Side 2: And Jacob's hip was put out of joint as he wrestled with him. *(Jacob stumbles but places hands on man's shoulders)*

Man: Let me go, for the day is breaking.

Jacob: I will not let you go, unless you bless me.

Man: What is your name?

Jacob: Jacob.

Man: You shall no longer be called Jacob *(Jacob takes hands off Man and puts them to his side)*, but Israel, for you have striven with God and with humans, and have prevailed.

Jacob: Please tell me your name.

Man: Why is it that you ask my name?

Both Sides: And there he blessed him. *(Man puts hand on Jacob's head, then removes hand and turns away from Jacob. Jacob turns forward)* So Jacob called the place Peniel, saying,

Jacob: For I have seen God face to face, and yet my life is preserved.

All: The sun rose upon him as he passed Peniel, limping because of his hip.

Matthew 14:13-21: *Use the same choral speaking choir. Several baskets of torn bread can be sitting on the altar or elsewhere in the chancel. Have the Man become Jesus and the rest will be disciples. The set-up — standing close to the top of the steps:*

```
        X X X X X
         X X X X
           Jesus
```

One Voice: When Jesus heard this, he withdrew from there in a boat to a deserted place by himself. *(Jesus turns facing backward)*

All: But when the crowds heard it, they followed him on foot from the towns. When he went ashore, he saw a great crowd; and he had compassion for them and cured their sick. *(Jesus lifts arms, and then puts them down)*

One Voice: When it was evening, the disciples came to him and said,

All Voices (except Jesus)**:** This is a deserted place, and the hour is now late; send the crowds away so that they may go into the villages and buy food for themselves.

Jesus: They need not go away; you give them something to eat.

All Voices: We have nothing here but five loaves and two fish.

Jesus: Bring them here to me. *(Choir takes baskets off altar and brings them to Jesus)*

One Voice: Then he ordered the crowds to sit down on the grass.

Another Voice: Taking the five loaves and the two fish, he looked up to heaven, and blessed and broke the loaves, and gave them to the disciples, and the disciples gave them to the crowds. *(Choir goes out and passes the baskets to the congregation. Have enough baskets that this won't take very long. When choir is finished passing baskets, come back to their positions with the leftovers)* And all ate and were filled; and they took up what was left over of the broken pieces, twelve baskets full.

All Voices: And those who ate were about 5,000 men, besides women and children.

Call to Offering
Today we have been fed as Jesus fed the 5,000. May our offering be used to feed the hungry and thirsty in this community and around the world.

Prayer of Dedication
Good and loving God, bless our gifts today as Jesus blessed the bread and the fish. May the good this offering brings increase twelvefold, and may there be gifts left over. In Jesus' name we pray. Amen.

Benediction
Leader: Jacob has been blessed; Jesus has fed the 5,000.
People: We have experienced stories of miracles today.
Leader: Go, be a miracle yourself this week for someone with whom you meet.
People: What can we do? Where, How, When?
Leader: God will show you the way. May the blessings of God, our Creator, Christ, our Savior, and the Spirit who sustains us, go with you all. Amen.

Choral Response
Open My Eyes That I May See

Proper 14
Ordinary Time 19
Pentecost 12

Genesis 37:1-4, 12-28   Psalm 105:1-6, 16-22, 45b
Romans 10:5-15   Matthew 14:22-33

Hymns
Sing Praise To God (NCH6, CBH59, UM126, PH483)
Immortal Love, Forever Full (NCH166, CBH629)
Here, O God, Your Servants Gather/Sekai No Tomo (NCH72, CBH7, PH465)
When The Storms Of Life Are Raging (CBH558, UM512)
O Sing A Song Of Bethlehem (NCH51, UM179, PH308)
Precious Lord, Take My Hand (CBH575, NCH472, UM474, PH404)
Guide Me, O Thou Great Jehovah (CBH582, NCH18, 19, UM127, PH281)
O Day Of God, Draw Nigh (PH452)

Anthems
Joseph And The Coat, Tammy Waldrop, Ring Out! Press, Narrator/2 to 3-octave handbells
How Lovely Are The Messengers, Felix Mendelssohn, SATB
Sing, Dance, Clap Your Hands, Ziegenhals, CGA, Unison/2-part
So Long, Joe!, Malmstrom and Calhoun, musical unison/2 part, flute, percussion, CGC33

Call to Worship
Leader: O give thanks to God, call on God's name, make known God's deeds among the people.
People: Sing praises to God — tell of all the wonderful works.
Leader: Glory in God's holy name; let the hearts of those who seek God rejoice.
People: We seek God and God's strength.
All: We seek God's presence continually.

Call to Confession
Paul tells us that everyone who calls on the name of the Lord shall be saved. Let us now confess our sins before God and ask forgiveness. Let us pray.

Prayer of Confession
Merciful and loving God, we come to you this morning asking you to hear our prayer. We confess that we don't think of you very often. We go about our daily lives as if we are completely in charge of our lives. We know that isn't so, and you remind us of that quite often, but we still continually fool ourselves. You are our creator, God, and we know that you have given us free will to pursue our lives, but we want to do your will. Help us to be ever aware that you walk with us, God — that you are always there to guide us and protect us. Give us courage to stand straighter against the contrariness of the world. Remind us to call upon you whenever we need guidance. Forgive us for forgetting about you. Amen.

Assurance of Pardon
In Romans 10, Paul tells us that if we confess with our lips that Jesus is Lord and believe in our hearts that God raised him from the dead, we are saved. Everyone who calls on the name of the Lord shall be saved. Alleluia! We are forgiven. Amen.

Scripture Readings
Genesis 37:1-4: *This passage, as well as the one from Matthew are two very dramatic stories, both having to do with lack of faith and wanting more from their lives. The Genesis passage is also about jealousy and what happens when brother is pitted against brother. The NRSV version also changes the coat of many colors that we know about to a "long robe with sleeves." While this is probably more correct, it will be hard to use those words with a congregation, because they will get caught up in that description and forget the story. Preface the story with the change so that they won't be surprised. This story could easily be acted out by one of the Sunday school classes. An older class might be able to come up with a modern situation to substitute for the ancient story. But the ancient story runs the gamut of human emotions. The cast includes a Narrator, Jacob, Joseph, many Brothers (girls can easily be substituted for any of these parts), a Man in Field, Brother Reuben, some Ishmaelites, Brother Judah, Midianite, and Traders. Props include a long-sleeved, brightly colored coat, shepherd's crooks, bread in pockets of brothers, packages and baskets for traders to carry, moneybag. When the reading begins, Jacob is standing over by the pulpit with the Joseph coat over his arm. Brothers, including Joseph, are on other side of chancel.*

Narrator: Jacob settled in the land where his father had lived as an alien, the land of Canaan. This is the story of the family of Jacob. Joseph, being seventeen years old, was shepherding the flock with his brothers; he was a helper to the sons of Bilhah and Zilpah, his father's wives; and Joseph brought a bad report of them to their father. *(Joseph walks over to father and whispers in his ear)* Now Israel loved Joseph more than any other of his children, because he was the son of his old age; and he had made him a long robe with sleeves. *(Jacob shakes his head and gives Joseph the coat, helps him put it on, gives him big hug)* But when his brothers saw that their father loved him more than all his brothers, they hated him, and could not speak peaceably to him. *(Brothers watch from afar, talk amongst themselves, and move farther away — behind the altar if possible)* Now his brothers went to pasture their father's flock near Shechem. And Israel said to Joseph,

Jacob (Israel): Are not your brothers pasturing the flock at Shechem? Come, I will send you to them.

Joseph: Here I am.

Jacob: Go now, see if it is well with your brothers and with the flock; and bring word back to me.

Narrator: So he sent him from the valley of Hebron. *(Joseph begins wandering the front of the sanctuary. Man comes from stage left)* He came to Shechem, and a man found him wandering in the fields; the man asked him,

Man: What are you seeking?

Joseph: I am seeking my brothers. Tell me, please, where they are pasturing the flock.

Man: They have gone away, for I heard them say, "Let us go to Dothan." *(Man walks off stage right. Joseph continues to walk in a round bout way toward his brothers)*

Narrator: So Joseph went after his brothers, and found them at Dothan. They saw him from a distance, and before he came near to them, they conspired to kill him.

2 Brothers: Here comes the dreamer.

Brother 3: Come now, let us kill him and throw him into one of the pits.

Brother 4: Then we shall say that a wild animal has devoured him,

All Brothers (except Reuben): Then we shall see what will become of his dreams.

Reuben: No, let us not take his life. Shed no blood; throw him into the pit *(Points to floor)* here in the wilderness, but lay no hand on him.

Narrator: Reuben thought that he might rescue him out of their hand and restore him to his father. *(Joseph walks happily up to his brothers)* So when Joseph came to his brothers, they stripped him of his robe, the long robe with sleeves that he wore; and they took him and threw him into a pit. *(Brothers roughly rip off coat and throw Joseph down behind altar)* The pit was empty; there was no water in it. Then they sat down to eat *(Brothers sit and pull bread out of pockets to eat)* And looking up they saw a caravan of Ishmaelites coming from Gilead *(Group of Traders comes from stage right and crosses in front of Brothers carrying packages and baskets)* with their camels carrying gum, balm, and resin, on their way to carry it down to Egypt.

Judah: What profit is it if we kill our brother and conceal his blood? Come let us sell him to the Ishmaelites, and not lay our hands on him, for he is our brother, our own flesh. *(Other Brothers nod and agree. Another convoy of Traders comes in from stage left)*

Narrator: When some Midianite traders passed by, they drew Joseph up, lifting out of the pit, and sold him to the Ishmaelites for twenty pieces of silver. *(Brothers lift Joseph out of pit, and take him to Traders. One Trader hands them the moneybag. Traders go off stage right with Joseph looking back at Brothers. They watch, some gleefully, others wondering if they did the right thing)* And they took Joseph to Egypt.

Matthew 14:22-33: *This passage is a familiar one and could be well done by a storyteller who would act it out. The choral speaking choir can also do it.*

```
            1 2 3 4
            5 6 P
             7 8              Jesus
```

All Voices: Immediately he made the disciples get into the boat and go on ahead to the other side, while he dismissed the crowds.

Voices 7 and 8: And after he had dismissed the crowds, he went up the mountain by himself to pray.

Voice 6: When evening came, he was there alone,

Voices 4 and 5: But by this time the boat, battered by the waves, was far from the land, for the wind was against them.

Voice 3: And early in the morning he came walking toward them on the sea.

Voice 2: But when the disciples saw him walking on the sea, they were terrified, saying,

All Voices: It is a ghost! *(Wail in fear)*

Voice 1: But immediately Jesus spoke to them and said,

Jesus: Take heart, it is I; do not be afraid.

Voice 8: Peter answered him,

Peter: Lord, if it is you, command me to come to you on the water.

Jesus: Come.

Voice 7: So Peter got out of the boat, started walking on the water, and came toward Jesus.

Voices 5 and 6: But when he noticed the strong wind, he became frightened, and beginning to sink, he cried out,

Peter: Lord, save me!

Voice 4: Jesus immediately reached out his hand and caught him, saying to him,

Jesus: You of little faith, why did you doubt? *(Walks over to rest of choir and joins them)*

Voice 3: When they got into the boat, the wind ceased.

Voice 2: And those in the boat worshiped him, saying,

All: Truly you are the Son of God.

Benediction (from the hymn *Sing Praise To God*)
Leader: Let all who name Christ's holy name give God all praise and glory.
People: Let all who own his power proclaim aloud the wondrous story!
Leader: Cast each false idol from its throne, for Christ is Lord, and Christ alone.
All: To God all praise and glory. Amen.

Proper 15
Ordinary Time 20
Pentecost 13

Genesis 45:1-15 **Psalm 133**
Romans 11:1-2a, 29-32 **Matthew 15:(10-20) 21-28**

Hymns
O Christ, The Healer, We Have Come (NCH175, CBH379, UM265, PH380)
Now Thank We All Our God (NCH419, CBH86, UM102, PH555)
How Good A Thing It Is (CBH310)
Behold The Goodness Of Our Lord (PH241)
All People That On Earth Do Dwell (LBW245, NCH7, PH220, 221, UM75, CBH42)
Help Us Accept Each Other (NCH388, PH358, UM560)
Where Charity And Love Prevail (LBW126, NCH396, UM549, CBH305)
In Christ There Is No East Or West (LBW359, NCH394, 395, PH439, 440, UM548, CBH306)

Anthems
O Lord, Increase My Faith, Orlando Gibbons, H. W. Gray, SATB
Behold, How Good And Joyful, Benjamin Rogers, Concordia, SATB
Make Music, Huff/Martin, CGA, Unison/2-part
Help Us Accept Each Other, arr. Hruby (Puerto Rican), Unison, optional flute, optional guitar

Call to Worship (based on Psalm 133)
Leader: How very good and pleasant it is when kindred live together in unity!
Men: It is like the precious oil on the head, running down upon the beard, on the beard of Aaron, running down over the collar of his robes.
Women: It is like the dew of Hermon, which falls on the mountains of Zion.
All: For there the Lord ordained his blessing, life forevermore.

Call to Offering
As God sent Joseph to Egypt to prepare for the coming famine, so God watches over each of us. Let us now confess to God our shortcomings and our sinful nature. Let us pray.

Prayer of Confession
Benevolent God, we come to you today to confess our jealous nature. We watch other people get the job we wanted, and our mouths spew hurtful comments. We malign our friends when we don't get our own way. We don't take the blame upon ourselves when our actions cause others to be hurt. Hardly a day goes by when we don't behave from our jealous nature rather than our loving one. Forgive us, God. Help us so that we don't behave like Joseph's brothers, resenting the love his father had for him. Help us to see the best in the people with whom we work and live. Be with the leaders of nations to work together for the best interests of all people. Show us your mercy. Amen.

Assurance of Forgiveness
Jesus Christ shows mercy to all who come asking for forgiveness, and who are truly repentant. Christ died for us; Christ lives for us. Alleluia! Amen.

Scripture Readings
Genesis 45:1-15: *This passage is best done by one person who has memorized the lesson, and can act it out. It can be read if done well, but it won't be nearly as effective. Have "Joseph" read this passage from the sanctuary floor, right in the middle of the congregation.*

Matthew 15:(10-20) 21-28: *This passage is best done with a choral speaking choir. Do not read verses 10-20, unless you plan to preach on them. Verses 21-28 are very effective alone.*

```
              4 5
             3   6
            2     W
           1       7
              J
```

All Voices: Jesus left that place and went away to the district of Tyre and Sidon.

Voice 7: Just then a Canaanite woman from that region *(Woman takes three steps toward Jesus)* came out and started shouting,

Woman: Have mercy on me, Lord, Son of David; my daughter is tormented by a demon.

Voice 1: But he did not answer her at all. And his disciples came and urged him, saying,

Voices 3, 4, 5, and 6: Send her away, for she keeps shouting after us.

Voice 2: He answered,

Jesus: I was sent only to the lost sheep of the house of Israel.

Voice 2: But she came and knelt before him, saying,

Woman: Lord, help me.

Voice 2: He answered,

Jesus: It is not fair to take the children's food and throw it to the dogs.

Voice 2: But she said,

Woman: Yes, Lord, yet even the dogs eat the crumbs that fall from their master's table.

Voice 1: Then Jesus answered her,

Jesus: Woman, great is your faith! Let it be done for you as you wish.

All Voices: And her daughter was healed instantly.

Call to Offering
May our offering today go to feed hungry children and heal the sick around the world. As the woman came to Jesus, knelt and said, "Lord, help me," may we help those who need our help.

Prayer of Dedication (from hymn *Where Charity And Love Prevail*)
Leader: Where charity and love prevail, there God is ever found,
People: Brought here together by Christ's love, by love are we thus bound.
Left Side: With grateful joy and holy fear true charity we learn;
Right Side: Let us with heart and mind and strength now love Christ in return. Amen.

Closing Hymn
Help Us Accept Each Other

Benediction
Leader: Help us accept each other with all of our warts and all of our gifts
People: Just as Christ accepted us.
Leader: Teach others to work together for the betterment of all humankind.
People: Just as Christ taught us.
Leader: Help us to learn from others better ways of being in the world
People: Just as we learned from Christ.
Leader: Be present, God, among us and bring us to believe that we are ourselves accepted,
All: And meant to love and live. Amen.

Proper 16
Ordinary Time 21
Pentecost 14

Exodus 1:8—2:10 Psalm 124
Romans 12:1-8 Matthew 16:13-20

Hymns
In Egypt Under Pharaoh (NCH574)
Christ Is Made The Sure Foundation (LBW367, NCH400, PH416, 417)
Like The Murmur Of The Dove's Song (NCH270, CBH29, UM544, PH314)
There Are Many Gifts (CBH304)
Una Espiga/Sheaves Of Summer (CBH460, NCH338, UM637, PH518)
Built On The Rock (CBH309)
Take My Life And Let It Be (UM399, NCH448, CBH389, PH391)
Lord, Whose Love Through Humble Service (PH427, CBH369, UM581)

Anthems
Upon This Rock, John Ness Beck, G. Schirmer, SATB/brass
To Do God's Will, Jean Berger, Augsburg, SATB
Like The Murmur Of The Dove's Song, White, CGA, Unison/2-part
Gifts Of Life, Printz, 2-part with flute

Call to Worship
Leader: Our help is in the name of the Lord, who made heaven and earth.
People: We come to give God thanks and praise.
Leader: Our help is in our Creator God, who made the day and the night.
People: Thanks be to the God of all creation.
Leader: Our help is in the God who created all humankind.
People: Let us worship the God who loves us all.

Call to Confession
Let us come together in prayer as we ask God for forgiveness for our human frailties and our deliberate sinfulness. Let us pray.

Prayer of Confession
Gracious God, we know that you have given each of us different abilities and gifts. We also know that we are to use those gifts in your service. In using our gifts to the fullest, we know that we can be transformed in our faithfulness. But so often we squander the gifts you have given us. Sometimes we fail to see the gifts you have given because we want so badly to have other gifts. We want to be great athletes and don't notice our gift of gab. Or we recognize the gift, but use it badly. That ability to talk and to convince others is used to put down other people, instead of building up your kingdom. Perhaps we have been told as children that our gifts aren't important ones, and we have grown to believe it. Strengthen us, O God, to appreciate our own special gifts. Forgive us for using them badly, or not using them at all. Help us honor who we are as your people. Walk with us, O God.

Assurance of Forgiveness
Just as God loves us and creates each of us as unique persons with special gifts, God also loves us so much that he gave each of us the greatest gift of all — himself. Jesus Christ gave the ultimate sacrifice so that each of us might live and be forgiven. We are so blessed. So live in faith. Amen.

Scripture Readings
Romans 12:1-8: *This passage is a good scripture for a younger Sunday school class, possibly first and second graders. The teacher could have the children gather around her/him on the steps to the chancel, possibly sitting around her/him. The class would have talked about this scripture so that the children would understand the concepts of each of us using our gifts to do God's work in the world. The teacher then would read Romans 12:1-6a. Then as the gifts are mentioned each child would stand up and say his/her line.*

Child 1: Prophecy, in proportion to faith;

Child 2: Ministry, in ministering;

Child 3: The teacher, in teaching;

Child 4: The exhorter, in exhortation; .

Child 5: The giver, in generosity;

Child 6: The leader, in diligence;

Child 7: The compassionate, in cheerfulness.

Matthew 16:13-20: *The choral speaking choir can do this passage.*

```
          1 2
         3 4 5
        6  Peter            Jesus
```

Voice 6: Now when Jesus came into the district of Caesarea Philippi, he asked his disciples,

Jesus: Who do people say that the Son of Man is?

Voice 6: And they said,

Voice 3: Some say John the Baptist,

Voice 4: Others say Elijah,

Voice 5: Still others Jeremiah or one of the prophets.

Voice 6: He said to them,

Jesus: But who do you say that I am?

Voice 1: Simon Peter answered,

Peter: You are the Messiah, the Son of the living God.

Voice 1: And Jesus answered him,

Jesus: Blessed are you, Simon son of Jonah! For flesh and blood has not revealed this to you, but my Father in heaven. And I tell you, you are Peter, and on this rock I will build my church, and the gates of Hades will not prevail against it. I will give you the keys of the kingdom of heaven, and whatever you bind on earth will be bound in heaven, and whatever you loose on earth will be loosed in heaven.

Voice 2: Then he sternly ordered the disciples

Voices 2, 3, 4: Not to tell anyone

All Voices: That he was the Messiah.

Call to Offering
Paul said to the people of Rome, "Do not be conformed to this world, but be transformed by the renewing of your minds, so that you may discern what is the will of God — what is good and acceptable and perfect." May our morning offering be good and acceptable in the eyes of our God.

Prayer of Dedication
Merciful God, we thank you for your many gifts to us. May the money we have given today lift up the body of Christ in the world, so that the gift you gave humanity can be seen and felt by the homeless, the poverty stricken, the motherless, and all those in need of your love. Risen Christ, we thank you. Amen.

Closing Hymn
Take My Life And Let It Be

Benediction
Leader: Share the gifts that God has given you.
People: May our lives be consecrated to you, O God.
Leader: Use your moments and your days to do God's work in the world.
People: Take our hands and let them do the work you would have us do.
All: May our lips be filled with messages from God.
Leader: In the name of God, our Creator, Christ our Redeemer, and the Holy Spirit, our Sustainer. Amen.

Proper 17
Ordinary Time 22
Pentecost 15

Exodus 3:1-15   Psalm 105:1-6, 23-26, 45c
Romans 12:9-21   Matthew 16:21-28

Hymns
When Israel Was In Egypt's Land (NCH572, UM448, CBH164, PH334)
The God Of Abraham Praise (NCH24, UM116, CBH162, PH488)
Go Down, Moses (NCH572, PH334)
We Shall Overcome (NCH570, UM533)
Nearer, My God, To Thee (NCH606, UM528)
Take Up Thy Cross (UM415, CBH536, PH393)
Here I Am, Lord (CBH395, UM593, PH525)
God Of Many Names (CBH77, UM105)
O Love That Will Not Let Me Go (CBH577, CBH480, NCH485, PH384)
Come Sing, O Church, In Joy (PH430)

Anthems
Before Your Cross, O Jesus, Steve Karin, Jeffers, 3-octave handbells
If Any Will Come After Me, David Stanley York, Mercury, SATB/B
Lord, Make Me An Instrument Of Thy Peace, Jody Lindh, CGA, SATB
Songs from The Puzzling Parables, Jordan/Zabel, CGC31, Unison/2-part

Call to Worship (based on Psalm 105)
Leader: O give thanks to God, call upon God's name, and tell everyone about God's great deeds.
People: Sing to God, sing praises — tell of all God's wonderful works.
Leader: Glory in God's holy name; let the hearts of those who see God rejoice.
People: Seek God's presence continually; seek God's strength.
All: Praise God!

Prayer of Invocation
Great and glorious God, when Moses came upon a burning bush which was not consumed, he stopped and had a conversation with you. Speak to us today, God, through this service. Help us to know what you would have us do to further your kingdom now. Grab our attention, God, as we listen to your word read and interpreted, as we sing the hymns and pray together. May we be attentive to the sound of your voice in this place. Amen.

Scripture Readings
Exodus 3:1-15: *This passage is perfect to be acted out by three middle school or high school students. The first two verses set the stage, and can be read by a Narrator. The rest of the passage is a conversation between God and Moses. Have the class create a burning bush (possibly a bush with red cellophane paper and light bulbs set inside — or perhaps simply a*

drawing placed in front of the lectern or pulpit). God can stand in the pulpit or be hidden behind it — with a microphone. Moses will be on the floor watching the sheep.

Narrator: Moses was keeping the flock of his father-in-law Jethro, the priest of Midian; he led his flock beyond the wilderness, and came to Horeb, the mountain of God. *(Moses wandering, comes close to the pulpit)* There the angel of the Lord appeared to him in a flame of fire out of a bush; he looked, and the bush was blazing; yet it was not consumed.

Moses: I must stop and look at this great sight, and see why the bush is not burned up.

God: Moses, Moses!

Moses: Here I am.

God: Come no closer! Remove the sandals from your feet, for the place on which you are standing is holy ground. *(Moses removes sandals and holds them in his hand)* I am the God of your father, the God of Abraham, the God of Isaac, and the God of Jacob. *(Moses turns away and hides his face)* I have observed the misery of my people who are in Egypt; I have heard their cry on account of their taskmasters. Indeed, I know their sufferings and I have come down to deliver them from the Egyptians, and to bring them up out of that land to a good and broad land, a land flowing with milk and honey, to the country of the Canaanites, the Hittites, the Amorites, the Perizzites, the Hivites, and the Jebusites. *(Moses turns back around, looking curious)* The cry of the Israelites has now come to me; I have also seen how the Egyptians oppress them. So come, I will send you to Pharaoh to bring my people, the Israelites, out of Egypt.

Moses: *(Jumps back and looks frightened)* Who am I that I should go to Pharaoh, and bring the Israelites out of Egypt?

God: I will be with you; and this shall be the sign for you that it is I who sent you: when you have brought the people out of Egypt, you shall worship God on this mountain.

Moses: *(Still looks confused and reluctant)* If I come to the Israelites and say to them, "The God of your ancestors has sent me to you," and they ask me, "What is his name?" what shall I say to them?

God: I AM WHO I AM. Say to the Israelites, "I AM has sent me to you." The LORD, the God of your ancestors, the God of Abraham, the God of Isaac, and the God of Jacob, has sent me to you. This is my name forever, and this my title for all generations.

Romans 12:9-21: *The Romans passage can be introduced from the pulpit, and then each verse might be read by someone on the congregation. This could be called a "Pop-Up Scripture," with the different members standing when it is their turn to read. This would be very effective, putting an emphasis on each verse and on what Paul was trying to get across in this passage. It also could be read as a responsive reading between the left and the right sides of the congregation.*

Matthew 16:12-28: *This passage could be interpreted by the same class as the Exodus passage, using the same Narrator and two other students to be Peter and Jesus. The rest of the class could be the disciples whom Jesus addresses. It is very easy to get the blocking directly from the passage. Jesus might stand in front of the altar in the middle of the chancel. The disciples would be both to his right and left, some sitting and some standing. Peter would come and take his arm and lead him a few steps away to talk to him. Jesus would then rebuke Peter and come back to the "teaching" place to finish.*

Call to Offering
In the Romans passage read today, Paul tells us to "rejoice with those who rejoice, weep with those who weep. Live in harmony with one another." May our morning offering show our solidarity with people all over the world who need our help. The ushers will now wait upon us.

Prayer of Dedication
Loving and giving God, we ask your blessing over our gifts this morning, and we give them over to your service. In giving of ourselves we understand that we receive the greatest gift, the gift of service. Amen.

Benediction

Leader: Let your love be genuine; hate what is evil; hold fast to what is good.
Left Side: Love one another with mutual affection.
Right Side: Outdo one another in showing honor.
Leader: Do not lag in zeal; be ardent in spirit; serve God.
Women: Rejoice in hope,
Men: Be patient in suffering.
All: Persevere in prayer.
Leader: Extend hospitality to strangers. In the name of God who loves us, Christ who saves us, and the Holy Spirit who works within us, go in peace. Amen.

Proper 18
Ordinary Time 23
Pentecost 16

Exodus 12:1-14 Psalm 149
Romans 13:8-14 Matthew 18:15-20

Hymns
Wake, Awake, For Night Is Flying (UM720, NCH112, PH17)
Draw Us In The Spirit's Tether (UM632, NCH337, PH504)
Spirit Of Jesus, If I Love My Neighbor (NCH590)
Savior God Above (NCH602)
God is Here! (NCH70, UM660, PH461)
Where Charity And Love Prevail (NCH396, UM549, CBH305)
Give Praise To The Lord (PH257)
The Day Of Resurrection (LBW141, NCH245, PH118, UM303)

Anthems
Cantate Domino, Pitoni, GIA, SATB
Cause Us, O Lord, Ron Nelson, Boosey and Hawkes, SATB
O Sing To The Lord/Cantad al Senor, Ziegenhals, CGA, Unison/2-part
And I Will Praise Him, Jothen, Unison/2-part

Call to Worship (based on Psalm 149)
If you have a director of music who could create a musical response to the words: "Praise the Lord! Sing to the Lord a new song," this would be a good way to start your worship service. Have the musician teach the response to the congregation before the service begins.
Leader: Praise the Lord! Sing to the Lord a new song, his praise in the assembly of the faithful.
People: *(Singing)* Praise the Lord! Sing to the Lord a new song.
Leader: Let the children of Zion rejoice. Let them praise God's name with dancing, making melody to God with tambourine and lyre.
People: *(Singing)* Praise the Lord! Sing to the Lord a new song.
Leader: For Yahweh takes pleasure in his people and adorns the humble with victory.
People: *(Singing)* Praise the Lord! Sing to the Lord a new song.
Leader: Let the faithful exult in glory; let them sing for joy!
All: *(Singing)* Praise the Lord! Sing to the Lord a new song.

Call to Confession
Where two or three are gathered in God's name, God is among them. Let us now confess our sins to the God who is among us, laying before God those things we have done which harm our relationship with this God among us.

Prayer of Confession
God among us, we come to worship you every week for many reasons. One is to be refreshed in spirit for the week to come. Another is because we're feeling guilty for things we have done or

not done to others. Another reason is because we want our children to learn decent values to live in this world. But very seldom do we come because we know in our hearts that you are here among us. In fact, you are with us all the time, but we don't remember to include you in our decision-making. Forgive us, God, for forgetting you. Help us to praise and glorify you for all good gifts, especially the gift of forgiveness and eternal life given to us through your son, Jesus Christ. Amen.

Assurance of Forgiveness
Loving God, throughout history you have given your people promises, and over and over we have forgotten them. But your greatest promise was Jesus Christ who promises to forgive our sins if we but only repent and ask for forgiveness. What great news for us. Thank you, God. Help us remember to ask. Amen.

Scripture Readings
Romans 13:8-14: *This passage would work well with a choral speaking choir.*

```
              4   6
            3       7
          2   5   8
        1           9
```

Voice 1: Owe no one anything, except to love one another; for the one who loves another has fulfilled the law. The commandments:

Voice 2: You shall not commit adultery;

Voice 5: You shall not murder;

Voice 8: You shall not steal;

Voice 3: You shall not covet;

Voice 1: Are summed up in this word,

All: Love your neighbor as yourself.

Voice 4: Love does no wrong to a neighbor; therefore,

All: Love is the fulfilling of the law.

Voice 9: Besides this, you know what time it is, how it is now the moment for you to wake from sleep. For salvation is nearer to us now than when we became believers

Voice 6: The night is far gone, the day is near. Let us lay aside the works of darkness and put on the armor of light.

Voice 7: Let us live honorably as in the day

Voices 3 and 7: Not in reveling and drunkenness

Voices 3, 5, and 7: Not in debauchery and licentiousness,

Voices 3, 5, 7, and 8: Not in quarreling and jealousy.

All: Instead, put on the Lord Jesus Christ, and make no provision for the flesh, to gratify its desires.

Matthew 18:15-20: *Again use the choral speaking choir.*

1	2
3	4
5	6
7	8

Voice 1: If another member of the church sins against you, go and point out the fault when the two of you are alone. *(Takes one step toward the other line)*

Voice 2: If the member listens to you, you have regained that one. *(Takes one step toward the other line)*

Voices 3, 5, and 7: But if you are not listened to, take one or two others along with you, so that every word may be confirmed by the evidence of two or three witnesses. *(Take one step toward the other line)*

Voices 4, 6, and 8: If the member refuses to listen to them, tell it to the church. *(Take one step toward the other line)*

All: And if the offender refuses to listen even to the church, let such a one be to you as a Gentile and a tax collector. *(Turn away from each other)*

Left Side: Truly I tell you, whatever you find on earth will be bound in heaven. *(Take one step toward the other line)*

Right Side: And whatever you loose on earth will be loosed in heaven. *(Take one step toward the other line. You should be standing next to each other)*

Voices 7 and 9: Again truly I tell you, if two of you agree on earth about anything you ask, it will be done for you by my Father in heaven.

All: For where two or three are gathered in my name, I am there among them.

Call to Offering
Leader: What time is it?
People: It is time to express our love for God by giving of ourselves with the morning offering.
Leader: Salvation is nearer to us now than when we became believers. Let us give generously and with love.

Benediction
Leader: You know what time it is, how it is now the moment for you to wake from sleep.
People: Salvation is nearer to us now that when we became believers.
Leader: The night is far gone; the day is here.
People: Let us lay aside the works of darkness and put on the armor of light.
Leader: Live honorably; put on Christ, go out into the world, and work in the light and love of Jesus. Amen.

Proper 19
Ordinary Time 24
Pentecost 17

Exodus 14:19-31 Psalm 114
Romans 14:1-12 Matthew 18:21-35

Hymns
Lord, Speak To Me (UM463, NCH531, PH426)
When We Are Living/Pues Si Vivimos (UM356, NCH499, PH400)
When Israel Was In Egypt's Land (CBH164, UM448, NCH572, PH334)
Come, Ye Faithful, Raise The Strain (CBH264, 265, UM315, NCH230, PH114, 115)
Wade In The Water (CBH446)
At The Name Of Jesus (CBH342, UM168, PH148)
Forgive Our Sins As We Forgive (CBH137, UM390, PH347)
Out Of Deep, Unordered Water (PH494)

Anthems
Who Is Like Our God?, Pete Sanchez, Jr., Hosanna!, *Music Songbook, 1,* p. 95
Have Mercy On Us, O My Lord, Aaron Copeland, Boosey and Hawkes, SATB
Help Us Accept Each Other, Hruby, CGA, Unison
Wade In The Water, arr. Exner, CGA, Unison

Call to Worship (based on Psalm 114)
Leader: Tremble, O earth, at the presence of the Lord, at the presence of the God of Jacob,
People: Who turns the rock into a pool of water, the flint into a spring of water.
Leader: Tremble, O earth, at the presence of God in this place.
People: We tremble and turn our hearts to worship God.

Call to Confession
God welcomes all who are weak in faith. So we come to this time of prayer confessing our weaknesses in our life to our God. Let us pray together.

Prayer of Confession
Forgiving and gracious God, we come to you today filled with shame at our weakness. We continually pass judgment on others. We find fault with everyone, but very seldom look at, or recognize our own faults. We refuse to forgive those who wrong us, even though we know that you are willing to forgive us. Even when we are begged to forgive someone, we remain righteous and unbent. Help us truly to forgive others, God. Help us to do more than say, "Oh, that's okay," and then remain with our hearts hardened against that person. Remind us of your grace, and help us to offer it to others. Amen.

Assurance of Forgiveness
The book of Romans tells us, "If we live, we live to the Lord, and if we die, we die to the Lord; so then, whether we live or whether we die, we are the Lord's. For to this end Christ died and

lived again, so that he might be Lord of both the dead and the living." Christ died for each of us in order that we might be forgiven. Alleluia! Amen.

Scripture Readings
Romans 14:1-12: *This passage can be read simply but dramatically. It is about passing judgment on others, and it needs to be read with emphasis.*

Matthew 18:21-35: *This passage, also about judgment, could be dramatized by a group of older elementary/middle school children. The cast would include a Narrator to introduce the passage, Peter, Jesus (who actually tells the parable), a King, a Bad Slave, Slave 2, and other Slaves. Narrator would be at the pulpit or lectern; Peter and Jesus in the middle of the staged area.*

Narrator: Then Peter came and said to Jesus,

Peter: Lord, if another member of the church sins against me, how often should I forgive? As many as seven times?

Jesus: Not seven times, but I tell you, seventy-seven times. For this reason the kingdom of heaven may be compared to a king *(King comes out stage right and stands in front of Peter and Jesus)* who wished to settle accounts with his slaves. *(Slaves standing in corner)* When he began the reckoning, one who owed him 10,000 talents was brought to him *(Slave comes over to King)*; and, as he could not pay, the king ordered him to be sold, together with his wife and children and all his possessions, and payment to be made. *(Slave falls at King's feet)* So the slave fell on his knees before him, saying,

Bad Slave: Have patience with me, and I will pay you everything.

Jesus: And out of pity, the lord of that slave released him and forgave him the debt. *(King bids man to rise, shakes hand and sends him away. Slave starts back to other Slaves, comes upon Slave 2)* But that same slave, as he went out, came upon one of his fellow slaves who owed him 100 denarii, and seizing him by the throat, he said,

Bad Slave: *(Grabbing Slave 2's throat)* Pay what you owe!

Jesus: Then his fellow slave fell down and pleaded with him,

Slave 2: *(Falling at his feet)* Have patience with me, and I will pay you.

Jesus: But he refused; then he went and threw him into prison *(Bad Slave puts Slave 2 off stage)* until he would pay the debt. When his fellow slaves saw what had happened *(other Slaves talk among themselves and walk over to King)*, they were greatly distressed, and they went and reported to their lord all that had taken place. Then his lord summoned him *(Bad Slave comes back to King)* and said to him,

King: You wicked slave! I forgave you all that debt because you pleaded with me. Should you not have had mercy on your fellow slave, as I had mercy on you?

Jesus: And in anger he handed him over to be tortured *(Fellow Slaves take Bad Slave off stage right and King walks off stage left)* until he would pay his entire debt. *(Jesus turns back to Peter)* So my heavenly Father will also do to every one of you, if you do not forgive your brother or sister from your heart.

Benediction
Leader: Judge not, lest you be judged, scripture tells us. How hard that is to do.
People: We must try to welcome people openly, without our own expectations getting in the way.
Leader: Go with forgiveness in your heart. Greet those you meet with the peace of Jesus Christ. Go in peace.
People: We pass the peace in this place, and go out to meet the world. Through Jesus Christ. Amen. *(Pass the peace among the congregation)*

Proper 20
Ordinary Time 25
Pentecost 18

Exodus 16:2-15 Psalm 105:1-6, 37-45
Philippians 1:21-30 Matthew 20:1-16

Hymns
Eat This Bread (CBH471, UM628)
Guide Me, O Thou Great Jehovah (CBH582, UM127, NCH18, 19, PH281)
Glorious Things Of Thee Are Spoken (CBH619, UM731, PH416, NCH307)
Sing Praise To God (NCH6, PH483, UM126, CBH59)
Before Your Cross, O Jesus (NCH191)
Come, Labor On (NCH532, PH415)
O Jesus, I Have Promised (LBW503, NCH493, PH388, 389, CBH447, UM396)
Lead On, O King Eternal (LBW495, NCH573, PH447, 448, UM580)

Anthems
What Is Life But Christ?, Philip Young, Broadman, SATB/trumpet
O Give Thanks Unto The Lord, Jean Berger, Hinshaw, SATB/div
Brethren, We Have Met To Worship, arr. Pethel, CGA, Unison/2-part or SATB
Sing Praise To God, Leaf, CGA, Unison

Call to Worship
Leader: Draw near to God. Come into God's sanctuary with singing.
People: With a voice of singing, we come to God's house filled with praise.
Leader: God is here and ready to hear our song.
People: Let us sing, "To God all praise and glory."

Opening Hymn
Sing Praise To God

Call to Confession
God heard the complaining of the Israelites when they were in the wilderness. He answered their cries of hunger with bread. God hears our complaining and answers us also, offering us forgiveness. Let us pray together, confessing our sins.

Prayer of Confession
Glorious God, we look around us and everywhere there are signs of your goodness, yet we don't see it. We are in too much of a hurry to listen to the bird in the tree or watch the dew sparkle on the grass. We must get somewhere: to work, to school, to exercise, to our chores. We don't take time to be with you, to tell you our problems, and to thank you for your goodness to us. We don't want to wait for anything, not even you, God. We are too full of ourselves and our wants — like the ancient Israelites, we don't put our trust in you. We only trust ourselves, and we're not even sure about that. Forgive us, God, for not knowing what is important — for not

spending time in prayer, for not seeing the bounty that you have given us. Help us slow down and put our trust in you, giver of all good gifts. Amen.

Assurance of Forgiveness
God has given us the greatest gift of all — his son, Jesus Christ. And in the gift he has shown us his great favor and his willingness to partner with us forever. Jesus Christ is our redeemer and by his death has given us the gift of forgiveness. Amen.

Scripture Readings
Exodus 16:2-15: *Use the choral speaking choir. In the pattern shown below, X represents the Israelites.*

```
                G
           X         X
          X           X
         X    M  A    X
         3             2
          X           X
           X         X
                1
```

Voice 1: The whole congregation of the Israelites set out from Elim; and Israel came to the wilderness of Sin, which is between Elim and Sinai, on the fifteenth day of the second month after they had departed from the land of Egypt. The Israelites said to them,

Israelites: If only we had died by the hand of the Lord in the land of Egypt, when we sat by the fleshpots and ate our fill of bread; for you have brought us out into this wilderness to kill this whole assembly with hunger.

Voice 2: Then the Lord said to Moses,

God: I am going to rain bread from heaven for you, and each day the people shall go out and gather enough for that day. In that way I will test them, whether they will follow my instruction or not. On the sixth day, when they prepare what they bring in, it will be twice as much as they gather on the other days.

Voice 3: So Moses and Aaron said to all the Israelites,

Moses and Aaron: In the evening you shall know that it was the Lord who brought you out of the land of Egypt, and in the morning you shall see the glory of the Lord, because he has heard your complaining against the Lord. For what are we, that you complain against us?

Voice 1: And Moses said,

Moses: When the Lord gives you meat to eat in the evening and your fill of bread in the morning, because the Lord has heard the complaining that you utter against him — what are we? Your complaining is not against us but against the Lord.

Voice 2: Then Moses said to Aaron,

Moses: Say to the whole congregation of the Israelites, "Draw near to the Lord, for he has heard your complaining."

Voice 3: And as Aaron spoke to the whole congregation of the Israelites, they looked toward the wilderness, and the glory of the Lord appeared in the cloud. The Lord spoke to Moses and said,

God: I have heard the complaining of the Israelites; say to them, "At twilight you shall eat meat, and in the morning you shall have your fill of bread; then you shall know that I am the Lord your God."

Voice 3: In the evening quails came up and covered the camp; and in the morning there was a layer of dew around the camp. When the layer of dew lifted, there on the surface of the wilderness was a fine flaky substance, as fine as frost on the ground.

Voice 1: When the Israelites saw it, they said to one another,

Israelites: What is it?

Voice 1: For they did not know what it was. Moses said to them,

Moses: It is the bread that the Lord has given you to eat.

Matthew 20:1-16: *Use the choral speaking choir, or the passage could also be done by one person dressed as Jesus, telling the parable.*

```
                5
             4     6
          3           7
       2                 8
    1        L             9
```

All: For the kingdom of heaven is like a landowner who went out early in the morning to hire laborers for his vineyard.

Voices 1, 2, and 3: After agreeing with the laborers for the usual daily wage, he sent them into his vineyard.

Voices 4, 5, and 6: When he went out about 9 o'clock, he saw others standing idle in the marketplace, and he said to them,

Landowner: You also go into the vineyard, and I will pay you whatever is right.

Voices 4, 5, and 6: So they went.

Voices 7, 8, and 9: When he went out again about noon and about 3 o'clock, he did the same.

Voice 1: And about 5 o'clock he went out and found others standing around; and he said to them,

Landowner: Why are you standing here idle all day?

Voice 2: They said to him,

All: Because no one has hired us.

Landowner: You also go into the vineyard.

Voice 3: When evening came, the owner of the vineyard said to his manager,

Landowner: Call the laborers and give them their pay, beginning with the last and then going to the first.

Voices 4, 5, and 6: When those hired about 5 o'clock came, each of them received the usual daily wage.

Voices 7, 8, and 9: Now when the first came, they thought they would receive more, but each of them also received the usual daily wage.

Voice 1: And when they received it, they grumbled against the landowner, saying,

Voices 2, 3, 4, 5, and 6: These last worked only one hour, and you have made them equal to us who have borne the burden of the day and the scorching heat.

Voice 7: But he replied to one of them,

Landowner: Friend, I am doing you no wrong. Did you not agree with me for the usual daily wage? Take what belongs to you and go; I choose to give to this last the same as I give to you. Am I not allowed to do what I choose with what belongs to me? Or are you envious because I am generous?

All Voices: So the last will be first, and the first will be last.

Call to Offering
The Israelites asked, and God brought quails, and gave them food from heaven in abundance, for God remembered his holy promise. Let us give of ourselves, in abundance.

Prayer of Dedication
Gracious God, accept the gifts we bring you today. May they be used to help people wandering in the wilderness of hunger, poverty, drought, and warfare. May they bring joy to people where there has been no joy. We ask this in the name of Jesus. Amen.

Benediction
Leader: Live your life worthy of the gospel of Jesus Christ.
People: We will stand firm in one spirit, striving side by side with one mind for the faith of the gospel.
Leader: Do not be intimidated by the prevailing culture. Go out as one of God's children.
People: We go out in joy to show God's love to the world.

Choral Response
I've Got The Joy, Joy, Joy, Joy Down In My Heart

Proper 21
Ordinary Time 26
Pentecost 19

Exodus 17:1-7   Psalm 78:1-4, 12-16
Philippians 2:1-13   Matthew 21:23-32

Hymns
At The Name Of Jesus (UM168, CBH342, PH148)
Creator Of The Stars Of Night (UM692, CBH177, PH4)
All Hail The Power Of Jesus' Name (CBH106, 285, UM154, NCH304, PH142, 143)
Jesus — The Very Thought Of Thee (NCH507, CBH588, UM175, PH310)
O Love, How Vast, How Flowing Free (NCH209, UM267, PH83)
Lift High The Cross (CBH321, UM159, NCH198, PH371)
Bless'd Be The Tie That Binds (CBH421, UM557, NCH393, PH438)
What Wondrous Love Is This (CBH530, UM292, NCH223, PH85)

Anthems
Let This Mind Be In You, Austin Lovelace, Warner Bros., SATB
Lord, I Lift Your Name On High, Betcher, Agape, 2 to 3-octave handbells
Creator Of The Stars Of Night, Ferguson, CGA, Unison
What A Wonder (Malasia*n*), arr. Hopson, CGA, Unison/2-part, optional 4 handbells

Call to Worship (based on Psalm 78)
Leader: Give ear, O people, to my teaching; incline your ears to the words of my mouth.
People: Open our ears that we might hear, voices of truth sent clear.
Leader: I will open my mouth in a parable; I will utter dark sayings from of old,
People: Things that we have heard and known, that our ancestors have told us.
Leader: We will not hide them from the children; we will tell to the coming generation the glorious deeds of God, and the wonders God has done.
People: Silently now we wait for God. Open our ears, illumine us, Spirit Divine.

Prayer of Invocation
God of wonder and might, throughout the ages you have done wonderful things for your people. You have provided food and drink, you have led us through the wilderness, you have walked with us through sadness and grief, and you have gifted us with the glory of your son Jesus Christ. Be with us today as we hear your word read and interpreted through song and sermon. May we be grateful to you and may we go from this place ready to share the good news. Amen.

Scripture Readings
Philippians 2:2-13: *This passage can either be read by one storyteller or by a choral speaking choir. It is an important passage, and one we have heard before many times. It is also a very emotional passage, and could easily be danced while it was being read. If you have access to a*

modern dancer, ask her to choreograph it to the reading of the words. If you have it danced, use only one speaker. If you use a choral speaking choir, a diagram of their positions follows:

```
              15 16
              13 14
        7 8 9 10 11 12
               5  6
               3  4
               1  2
```

All Voices: If then there is any encouragement in Christ, any consolation from love, any sharing in the Spirit, any compassion and sympathy, make my joy complete: be of the same mind, be of one accord, and of one mind.

Voice 1: Do nothing from selfish ambition or conceit, but in humility regard others as better than yourselves.

Voice 2: Let each of you look not to your own interests, but to the interests of others.

All Voices: Let the same mind be in you that was in Christ Jesus.

Voices 3 and 4: Who, though he was in the form of God, did not regard equality with God as something to be exploited,

Voices 5 and 6: But emptied himself, taking the form of a slave, being born in human likeness.

Voices 7, 8, 9, 10, 11, and 12: And being found in human form, he humbled himself and became obedient to the point of death

Voice 13: Even death on a cross.

Voices 14, 15, and 16: Therefore God also highly exalted him and gave him the name that is above every name,

Voices 1, 2, 3, 4, 5, 6, 13, 14, 15, and 16: So that at the name of Jesus every knee should bend, in heaven and on earth and under the earth,

All: And every tongue should confess that Jesus Christ is Lord, to the glory of God the Father.

Voices 1, 2, 3, 4, 5, 6, 7, and 8: Therefore, my beloved, just as you have always obeyed me, not only in my presence, but much more now in my absence, work out your own salvation with fear and trembling;

Voices 9, 10, 11, 12, 13, 14, 15, and 16: For it is God who is at work in you, enabling you both to will and to work for his good pleasure.

Matthew 21:23-32: *If you used a choral speaking choir for the Philippians passage, then have five members stay in the chancel. This passage can be done by five senior highs, also. You will need a Narrator, Jesus, and three Priests and Elders. Jesus will be standing on the top step looking out at the congregation. Narrator will be at the lectern, three Priests standing five or six steps behind Jesus and to the right.*

Narrator: When he entered the temple, the chief priests and the elders of the people came to him *(Priests walk toward Jesus)* as he was teaching, and said,

Priest 1: By what authority are you doing these things?

Priests 2 and 3: Who gave you this authority?

Jesus: *(Turns a little to look at them)* I will also ask you one question; if you tell me the answer, then I will also tell you by what authority I do these things. *(Priests look taken aback)* Did the baptism of John come from heaven, or was it of human origin?

Narrator: And they argue with one another.

Priest 2: If we say, "From heaven," he will say to us, "Why then did you not believe him?"

Priest 3: But if we say, "Of human origin," we are afraid of the crowd; for all regard John as a prophet.

Narrator: So they answered Jesus,

All Priests: We don't know.

Jesus: Neither will I tell you by what authority I am doing these things. *(Turns back to crowd)* What do you think? A man had two sons; he went to the first and said, "Son, go and work in the vineyard today." The son answered, "I will not," but later he changed his mind and went. The father went to the second and said the same; and he answered, "I go, sir"; but he did not go. Which of the two did the will of his father?

All Priests: The first son.

Jesus: Truly I tell you, the tax collectors and the prostitutes are going into the kingdom of God ahead of you. For John came to you in the way of righteousness and you did not believe him, but the tax collectors and the prostitutes believed him; and even after you saw it, you did not change your minds and believe him. *(Jesus walks down the steps and down the center aisle. The Priests cross their arms and say quietly, "Well, I never ..." and walk off right)*

Benediction
It is God who is at work in you, enabling you both to will and to work for God's good pleasure. Go and do the work of God in the world. In the name of God, our generous and loving parent, and Jesus, our mediator and friend, and through the energy of the Holy Spirit. Amen.

Proper 22
Ordinary Time 27
Pentecost 20

Exodus 20:1-4, 7-9, 12-20   Psalm 19
Philippians 3:4b-14   Matthew 21:33-46

Hymns
Cantemos al Senor (O Sing To The Lord) (UM149, CBH55, NCH39, PH472)
O Day Of Rest And Gladness (CBH641, NCH66)
From All That Dwell Below The Skies (CBH49, UM101, NCH27, PH229)
All Beautiful The March Of Days (CBH159, NCH434, PH292)
Awake My Soul (CBH609, NCH491)
When I Survey The Wondrous Cross (NCH224, CBH259, 260, UM298, 299, PH100, 101)
When Jesus Wept (NCH191, CBH234, PH312)
Be Thou My Vision (PH330, NCH451, CBH545, UM451)
God's Law Is Perfect And Gives Life (PH167)

Anthems
The Holy Ten Commandments, Josef Haydn, Mercury, 3 to 5 equal voices
The Heavens Are Telling, Josef Haydn, G Schirmer, SATB, with STB solos
God Called Moses, John Horman, CGA, Unison
O Sing To The Lord, Cantad al Senor, arr. Ziegenhals, CGA, Unison/2-part, optional maracas

Call to Worship (based on Psalm 19)
Leader: The heavens are telling the glory of God,
People: The firmament proclaims God's handiwork.
Leader: Day to day pours forth speech;
People: Night to night declares knowledge.
Leader: There is no speech, nor are there words; their voice is not heard;
People: Yet their voice goes out through all the earth,
All: Their words to the end of the world.

Prayer of Invocation
We call to you, O God. You have given us laws that we are to keep. And yet you sent your son to show us that some laws can and should be broken. Give us insight as we hear the ancient laws read and interpreted. Help us to know which laws are God-given, and which have been created out of human need or greed. Grant us wisdom as we listen to your word for us today. Amen.

Scripture Readings
Exodus 20:1-4, 7-9, 12-20: *This passage can be strengthened by having an amplified voice read the Ten Commandments without the congregation being able to see that person. It can be very effective if you have someone with a good and authoritative voice. The sex of the person does not matter as long as he/she speaks confidently. Have a Narrator at the lectern, and have people in the congregation stand up and read together the People's part.*

Narrator: Then God spoke all these words:

God: I am the Lord your God, who brought you out of the land of Egypt, out of the house of slavery; you shall have no other gods before me. You shall not make for yourself an idol, whether in the form of anything that is in heaven above, or that is on the earth beneath, or that is in the water under the earth. You shall not make wrongful use of the name of the Lord your God, for the Lord will not acquit anyone who misuses his name. Remember the sabbath day, and keep it holy. Six days you shall labor and do all your work. Honor thy father and your mother, so that your days may be long in the land that the Lord your God is giving you. You shall not murder. You shall not commit adultery. You shall not steal. You shall not bear false witness against your neighbor. You shall not covet your neighbor's house; you shall not covet your neighbor's wife, or male, or female slave, or ox, or donkey, or anything that belongs to your neighbor.

Narrator: When all the people witnessed the thunder and lightning, the sound of the trumpet, and the mountain smoking, they were afraid and trembled and stood at a distance, and said to Moses,

People: You speak to us, and we will listen; but do not let God speak to us, or we will die.

Narrator: Moses said to the people, "Do not be afraid; for God has come only to test you and to put the fear of him upon you so that you do not sin."

Psalm 19: *This is a wonderful psalm, and makes mention of God's precepts. Use it in the service, and have the congregation read it responsively. The right side would read the odd-numbered verses and the left side the even-numbered verses. A deaf sign language interpreter might stand at the front of the church and sign it as the people read and watch the interpretation.*

Matthew 21:33-46: *This passage is very violent, so do not act it out. But it is an important passage as it is also about the Law and the Pharisees' interpretation of the Law. It is definitely a warning to the Pharisees. One person could read it, as Jesus taught, or it could be quite effective read by a choral speaking choir.*

```
            1 2 3
            4 5 6        10 11
            7 8 9           12
```

All: Listen to another parable.

Voice 7: There was a landowner who planted a vineyard, put a fence around it, dug a wine press in it, and built a watchtower.

Voice 8: Then he leased it to tenants and went to another country.

Voice 9: When the harvest time had come, he sent his slaves to the tenants to collect his produce.

Voices 10, 11, and 12: But the tenants seized his slaves and beat one, killed another, and stoned another.

All: And again he sent other slaves, more than the first;

Voices 10, 11, and 12: And they treated them in the same way.

Voice 4: Finally he sent his son to them, saying, "They will respect my son."

Voice 5: But when the tenants saw the son, they said to themselves,

Voices 1, 2, and 3: This is the heir; come, let us kill him and get his inheritance.

Voices 10, 11, and 12: So they seized him, threw him out of the vineyard, and killed him.

Voice 6: Now when the owner of the vineyard comes, what will he do to those tenants?

Voice 1: They said to him,

Voices 1 to 9: He will put those wretches to a miserable death, and lease the vineyard to other tenants who will give him the produce at the harvest time.

Voice 2: Jesus said to them,

Voice 3: Have you never read in the scriptures: "The stone that the builders rejected has become the cornerstone; this was the Lord's doing, and it is amazing in our eyes?"

Voice 4: Therefore I tell you, the kingdom of God will be taken away from you

Voices 5 and 6: And given to a people that produces the fruits of the kingdom.

Voices 7, 8, and 9: The one who falls on this stone will be broken to pieces;

Voices 1 to 9: And it will crush anyone on whom it falls.

Voices 10, 11, and 12: When the chief priests and the Pharisees heard his parables, they realized that he was speaking about them. They wanted to arrest him,

Voices 7 to 12: But they feared the crowds,

All: Because they regarded him as a prophet.

Call to Offering
In Philippians 3, Paul says that he presses on toward the goal for the prize of the heavenly call of God in Jesus Christ. May we all push on toward that goal as the ushers wait upon us for our gifts and offerings.

Prayer of Dedication
Great and awesome God, may the gifts we bring today be used to comfort the afflicted and to afflict the comforted as we press on toward the goal of your kingdom on earth. Amen.

Benediction
Leader: Go from this place today striving to keep God's laws. Let all your words and thoughts be as God would have them be, and show the love of God in all you do and say. Be kind yet brave in all your actions, and fear not, for God is with you. Amen.

Choral Response
God's Law Is Perfect (v. 1)

Proper 23
Ordinary Time 28
Pentecost 21

Exodus 32:1-14 Psalm 106:1-6, 19-23
Philippians 4:1-9 Matthew 22:1-14

Hymns
Rejoice, Ye Pure In Heart (UM160, 161, NCH55, 71, PH145, 146, LBW553)
Where Cross The Crowded Ways Of Life (UM427, CBH405, NCH543, PH408)
Sweet Hour Of Prayer (CBH11, UM496, NCH505)
Rejoice, The Lord Is King! (CBH288, UM716, NCH303, PH155)
What A Friend We Have In Jesus (NCH506, CBH573, UM526, PH403)
I Would Be True (NCH492)
Lead On, O King Eternal (LBW495, NCH573, PH447, 448, UM580)
We Come As Guests Invited (PH517)

Anthems
O Give Thanks To The Lord, John Bell, from *Enemy of Apathy,* GIA, Unison/SATB
Rejoice, Ye Pure In Heart, arr. Karen Buckwalter, Flammer, 3 to 5-octave handbells, optional brass and congregation
Sing And Speak Of God's Glory: Hymns, Scriptures And Responses, Helen Kemp, CGA, Unison/2-part
Blessing, Natalie Sleeth, CGA, Unison

Call to Worship (based on Psalm 106)
Leader: Praise God! Give thanks to God for he is good.
People: God's steadfast love endures forever!
Leader: Who can utter the mighty doings of Yahweh, or declare all praise?
People: Happy are those who observe justice, who do righteousness at all times.
All: Remember us, God, when you show favor to your people. May we glory in your heritage.

Call to Confession
God's people have been making mistakes and deliberately sinning since the dawn of creation. Let us confess our sins before the God who made us and knows what we have done. Let us pray.

Prayer of Confession
Mighty God, it must be so difficult for you to watch us continuing to pay no heed to your word. We read of the mistakes of the ancient Israelites as they let fear take over when Moses was gone. Even Moses' brother could not stem the tide of fear and resentment and they built that golden calf. And we can't get it right, either. Please forgive us for the times this past week when we let fear, or desire, or power, or greed get in the way of our relationship with you. We are your people, God, and we know it. But sometimes it is just so much easier to do what our friends suggest. We don't even know the person we're cheating or hurting. But you know what we're doing, God. Please stay steadfast in your love for us, and we'll keep on trying to get it right. Amen.

Assurance of Forgiveness
If we look, we can see the good news all around us. Remember? Jesus Christ loved us so much that he died to save us from all our sins! What a great gift. God really does love us! Alleluia! In Christ we are forgiven.

Scripture Readings
Exodus 32:1-14: *Give this passage to a class of eleven to thirteen-year-olds and have them create a drama from this passage. The subject is something they deal with every day in school and with friends and family — having the patience to let God do God's work. It also shows that one can argue with God and God will listen to you. The young people could modernize this passage, or they could do it directly from the Bible with their own "spin" on the story and their own modern touches. If you don't trust this process, then try having it read by five storytellers: God, Moses, Aaron, Narrator, and the People.*

Narrator: When the people saw that Moses delayed to come down from the mountain, the people gathered around Aaron, and said to him,

People: Come, make gods for us, who shall go before us; as for this Moses, the man who brought us up out of the land of Egypt, we do not know what has become of him.

Aaron: Take off the gold rings that are on the ears of your wives, your sons, and your daughters, and bring them to me.

Narrator: So all the people took off the gold rings from their ears, and brought them to Aaron. He took the gold from them, formed it in a mold, and cast an image of a calf; and they said,

People: These are your gods, O Israel, who brought you up out of the land of Egypt!

Narrator: When Aaron saw this, he built an altar before it; and Aaron made proclamation and said,

Aaron: Tomorrow shall be a festival to the Lord.

Narrator: They rose early the next day, and offered burnt offerings and brought sacrifices of well-being; and the people sat down to eat and drink, and rose up to revel. God said to Moses,

God: Go down at once! Your people whom you brought up out of the land of Egypt have acted perversely; they have been quick to turn aside from the way that I commanded them; they have cast for themselves an image of a calf, and have worshiped it and sacrificed to it, and said, "These are your gods, O Israel, who brought you up out of the land of Egypt!" I have seen this people, how stiff-necked they are. Now let me alone, so that my wrath may burn hot against them and I may consume them; and of you I will make a great nations.

Narrator: But Moses implored his God, and said,

Moses: O Lord, why does your wrath burn hot against your people, whom you brought out of the land of Egypt with great power and with a mighty hand? Why should the Egyptians say, "It was with evil intent that he brought them out to kill them in the mountains, and to consume them from the face of the earth"? Turn from your fierce wrath; change your mind and do not bring disaster on your people. Remember Abraham, Isaac, and Israel, your servants, how you swore to them by your own self, saying to them, "I will multiply your descendants like the stars of heaven, and all this land that I have promised I will give to your descendants, and they shall inherit it forever."

Narrator: And God changed his mind about the disaster that he planned to bring on his people.

Psalm 106:1-6, 9-12, 19-23: *If the Exodus passage has been used, the Psalm should be read responsively or by a choral speaking choir because it retells the Exodus story liturgically. As a responsive reading alternate between Leader and Congregation or divide the congregation to read alternately.*

Philippians 4:1-19: *This passage would gain most meaning when done by a storyteller who portrays Paul. It could also be read from the pulpit; or the leader could read verses 1-3 from the pulpit and have the congregation join in on verses 4-9.*

Benediction
All: Rejoice in the Lord, always.
Leader: Let your gentleness be known to everyone. God is close by. Do not worry, but let your requests be made known to God through prayer and supplication with thanksgiving. And the peace of God, which surpasses all understanding, will guard your hearts and your minds in Christ Jesus. Amen.

Choral Response
Rejoice In The Lord Always, And Again I Say Rejoice (found in most children's curriculum)

Proper 24
Ordinary Time 29
Pentecost 22

Exodus 33:12-23 **Psalm 99**
1 Thessalonians 1:1-10 **Matthew 22:15-22**

Hymns
In The Rifted Rock I'm Resting (CBH526)
A Wonderful Savior Is Jesus (CBH598)
God Whose Giving Knows No Ending (NCH565, CBH383, PH422)
O God Of Earth And Altar (NCH582, PH291, LBW428)
Take My Life And Let It Be (NCH448, CBH389, UM399, PH391)
Soplo de Dios Viviente/Breath Of The Living God (NCH56)
Lift Every Voice And Sing (LBW562, NCH593, PH563, UM519, CBH579)
God Is Here! (NCH70, PH461, UM660)

Anthems
With A Voice Of Singing, Martin Shaw, G. Schirmer, SATB
The Lord Is King, Francis A. Wapen, GIA, SAB
Lift Every Voice, Wilson, CGA, 2-part, optional handbells
God Of The Universe, Christopherson, CGA, 2-part, optional flute, percussion, Orff instruments

Call to Worship (based on Psalm 99)
Leader: Let the peoples tremble! God sits enthroned upon the cherubim; let the earth quake!
People: God is great in Zion, and is exalted over all the peoples.
All: Let us praise your great and awesome name. Holy is God!

Prayer of Invocation
Gracious and humbling God, we wish we could see you and know that you are there. But we also tremble before so great a countenance and are content with knowing you are with us. Fill us with your glory as we worship together. Give us the Holy Spirit to keep our energy fresh to worship you and to tell others about your goodness. In Jesus' name we pray. Amen.

Scripture Readings
Exodus 33:12-23; Psalm 99: *The Exodus passage and the Psalm can be read continuously. The congregation will have a part in it. Have the congregation open their Bibles to Psalm 99 and to be prepared to read when it is their turn, which is indicated by Left Side and Right Side. Use a choral speaking choir, also.*

1 2	7 8
3 4	9 10
5 6	11 12

Voice 5: Moses said to the Lord,

Voices 1-6: See, you have said to me, "Bring up this people"; but you have not let me know whom you will send with me. Yet you have said, "I know you by name, and you have also found favor in my sight." Now if I have found favor in your sight, show me your ways, so that I may know you and find favor in your sight. Consider too that this nation is your people.

Voice 12: God said,

Voices 7-12: My presence will go with you, and I will give you rest.

Voice 6: And Moses said to him,

Voices 1-6: If your presence will not go, do not carry us up from here. For how shall it be known that I have found favor in your sight, I and your people, unless you go with us? In this way, we shall be distinct, I and your people, from every people on the face of the earth.

Voice 11: God said to Moses,

Voices 7-12: I will do the very thing that you have asked; for you have found favor in my sight, and I know you by name.

Voice 3: Moses said,

Voices 1-6: Show me your glory, I pray.

Voice 10: And God said,

Voices 7-12: I will make all my goodness pass before you and will proclaim before you the name, "Yahweh," and I will be gracious to whom I will be gracious, and will show mercy on whom I will show mercy. But you cannot see my face; for no one shall see me and live. See, there is a place by me where you shall stand on the rock; and while my glory passes by I will put you in a cleft of the rock, and I will cover you with my hand until I have passed by; then I will take away my hand, and you shall see my back; but my face shall not be seen.

Right Side: The Lord is king; let the peoples tremble! He sits enthroned upon the cherubim; let the earth quake.

Left Side: The Lord is great in Zion; he is exalted over all the peoples.

Right Side: Let them praise your great and awesome name. Holy is he!

Left Side: Mighty King, lover of justice, you have established equity; you have executed justice and righteousness in Jacob.

All: Extol the Lord our God; worship at his footstool. Holy is he!

Voices 1-6: Moses and Aaron were among his priests, Samuel also was among those who called on his name. They cried to the Lord, and he answered them.

Voices 7-12: He spoke to them in the pillar of cloud; they kept his decrees, and the statutes that he gave them.

All: O Lord our God, you answered them; you were a forgiving God to them, but an avenger of their wrongdoings. Extol the Lord our God, and worship at his holy mountain; for the Lord our God is holy.

Matthew 22:15-22: *A storyteller might do the Matthew passage. It is short and familiar and could easily be memorized. Some of the verses have even come into modern vernacular.*

Call to Offering
Jesus said, "Render to Caesar what is Caesar's, and render to God the things that are God's." Let us now bring our gifts and offerings to do God's work into the world. The ushers will wait upon us for the morning offering.

Prayer of Dedication
Loving God, sometimes the best way for people to know you is from knowing people who do your work. May this offering be used today to help those who provide food for the hungry, housing for the homeless, care for the sick and suffering, and help the unemployed to find meaningful work. Help the helpless to see your face in this way. Amen.

Benediction
Leader: God, as you went with the people of Israel through the wilderness and into the promised land, go with us into our own wilderness of a people and a culture that don't know you. May God our Creator give us fortitude, Jesus our Redeemer be our guide, and the energy of the Holy Spirit carry us through until we meet again. Peace be with you.

People: And also with you. *(Pass the peace)*

Choral Response
Go With Us, Lord (PH535)

Proper 25
Ordinary Time 30
Pentecost 23

Deuteronomy 34:1-12   **Psalm 90:1-6, 13-17**
1 Thessalonians 2:1-8   **Matthew 22:34-46**

Hymns
O God, Our Help In Ages Past (CBH328, NCH25, UM117, LBW320, PH210)
Lord Of Our Growing Years (CBH479, PH279)
On Jordan's Stormy Banks I Stand (CBH610, NCH598, UM724, PH10)
Un Mandamiento Nuevo/Jesus A New Commandment (NCH389)
O Jesus Christ, May Grateful Hymns (NCH212, CBH404, PH424)
Spirit Of God, Descend Upon My Heart (NCH290, CBH502, UM500, LBW486, PH326)
Eternal God, Whose Power Upholds (PH412)
Come My Way, My Truth, My Life (LBW513, NCH331, UM164, CBH587)

Anthems
Precious Lord, Take My Hand, Roy Ringwald, Shawnee, SATB
O God, Our Help In Ages Past, Alan Hovhaness, C. F. Peters, SATB
I Will Love The Lord, Michael Bedford, CGA, Unison/2-part
To The Glory Of Our King, Robert Leaf, CGA, Unison

Call to Worship
Leader: Lord, you have been our dwelling place in all generations.
Men: Before the mountains were brought forth
Women: Or ever you had formed the earth and the world,
People: From everlasting to everlasting you are God.
Leader: Let the favor of the Lord our God be upon us,
People: And prosper for us the work of our hands,
All: O prosper the work of our hands! Amen.

Call to Confession
God knows who we are and what we do even before we know it ourselves. And yet we need to stand before God as God's people and confess our sins together, knowing that we cannot be perfect people. Let us pray together, asking for forgiveness.

Prayer of Confession
Oh Lord, how long? Your people have been asking this question forever. The ancient Israelites asked it as Moses led them across the desert. The psalmists wrote of both personal and corporate sufferings. The early Christians asked it on a daily basis, and still there are people suffering. We ask it, God. How long must we be sick or have loved ones who are ill? How long must we grieve? How long must we send our young men and women to war? How long must there be people sleeping on the street, children starving, and men and women dying from fatal diseases? We know much of the world's suffering comes from people, O God. We turn our backs on

others, thinking too much of ourselves. We waste resources and plunder the earth. We don't love each other as you would have us love. Forgive us, God. Help us to look around, see the injustices, and work toward peace in your world. How long, O Lord, will we need to be forgiven? Amen.

Assurance of Forgiveness
Jesus was asked, "How many times should we forgive another?" and he replied seventy times seven. God forgives us every time we sin if we repent and turn to Jesus for strength. Jesus was born for us, died for us, rose again for us. Alleluia! Our sins have been forgiven.

Scripture Readings
Psalm 90:1-6, 13-17: *The Pslam can be read in addition to either the Deuteronomy text or the Matthew text. Have the choral speaking choir read the Psalm; they should stand in a straight line across the chancel.*

1 2 3 4 5 6 7 8 9

All Voices: Lord, you have been our dwelling place in all generations.

Voices 1-3: Before the mountains were brought forth,

Voices 4-6: Or ever you had formed the earth and the world,

Voices 7-9: From everlasting to everlasting

All: You are God.

Voices 1-5: You turn us back to dust, and say,

Voices 6-9: Turn back, you mortals.

All: For a thousand years in your sight are like yesterday when it is past, or like a watch in the night.

Voices 1-5: You sweep them away; they are like a dream, like grass that is renewed in the morning;

Voices 6-9: In the morning it flourishes and is renewed; in the evening it fades and withers.

All: Turn, O Lord! How long? Have compassion on your servants!

Voices 1-3: Satisfy us in the morning with your steadfast love, so that we may rejoice and be glad all our days.

Voices 4-6: Make us glad as many days as you have afflicted us, and as many years as we have seen evil.

Voices 7-9: Let your work be manifest to your servants, and your glorious power to their children.

All: Let the favor of the Lord our God be upon us, and prosper for us the work of our hands — O prosper the work of our hands!

Matthew 22:34-46: *This passage has the Pharisees testing Jesus. It could be done by the choral speaking choir acting as the Pharisees, gathered in a semicircle around Jesus, like this:*

```
          4 5
         3   6
         2   7
         1   8
           J
```

All Voices: When the Pharisees heard that Jesus had silenced the Sadducees, they gathered together,

Voice 1: And one of them, a lawyer, asked him a question to test him,

Voice 8: Teacher, which commandment in the law is the greatest?

Voice 2: Jesus said to him,

Jesus: You shall love the Lord your God with all your heart, and with all your soul, and with all your mind. This is the greatest and first commandment. And a second is like it: You shall love your neighbor as yourself. On these two commandments hang all the law and the prophets.

Voice 7: Now while the Pharisees were gathered together, Jesus asked them this question:

Jesus: What do you think of the Messiah? Whose son is he?

Voice 3: They said to him,

All Voices: The son of David.

Voice 6: He said to them,

Jesus: How is it then that David by the Spirit calls him Lord, saying, "The Lord said to my Lord, 'Sit at my right hand, until I put your enemies under your feet' "? If David thus calls him Lord, how can he be his son?

Voices 4 and 5: No one was able to give him an answer,

All Voices: Nor from that day did anyone dare to ask him any more questions.

Benediction
Leader: Share the gospel of Jesus Christ in all you do and say; share yourselves with those whom you meet. Don't let fear of the unknown overtake you. Be brave and loving in all circumstances, and know that God is with you always. Amen.

All Saints' Sunday

Revelation 7:9-17　　Psalm 34:1-10, 22
1 John 3:1-3　　Matthew 5:1-12

Hymns
Crown Him With Many Crowns (NCH301, UM327, CBH116, PH151)
Blessed Assurance (NCH473, UM369, CBH332, PH341)
Lift High the Cross (NCH198, UM159, CBH321, PH371)
Dona Nobis Pacem (CBH346, UM376)
You Servants Of God (UM181, NCH305, PH477)
All Hail The Power Of Jesus' Name (CBH106, PH142, 143, UM154, 155, NCH304)
The King Of Love My Shepherd Is (CBH170, PH171, UM138, NCH248)
Jesus Shall Reign (CBH319, PH423, UM157, NCH300)
Lord, I Want To Be A Christian (PH372, CBH444, UM402, NCH454)
For All The Saints (PH526, CBH636, UM711, NCH299, LBW174)
I Sing A Song Of The Saints Of God (PH364, UM712, NCH295)

Anthems
Jerusalem, My Happy Home, K. Koschke, Morningstar, SATB
O Taste And See, Ralph Vaughn Williams, Oxford, SATB
Illumined By Your Light, Clemens, CGA, SATB
I Will Rejoice In The Lord, Telemann/Schoenfeld, CGA, 2-part

Call to Worship (based on Psalm 34)
Leader: I will bless God at all times; God's praise shall continually be in my mouth.
People: O magnify Yahweh together; let us exalt God's name.
Leader: I sought Yahweh, and I was answered; Yahweh delivered me from all my fears.
People: Look to God, and be radiant; so your faces shall never be ashamed.
All: O taste and see that the Lord is good; happy are those who take refuge in Yahweh.

Litany for the Saints of God
Leader: Today we pay homage to all those who have gone before us, who have given honor to their faith and who have lived lives as God-fearing people.

Voice 1: We give honor to our forebears in faith, those who walked with God and gave us our beginnings: Abraham, Isaac, Shiprah, Puah, Moses, Joshua, Deborah, David, and all those we hear about in the Old Testament.

Congregation: God, we give you thanks and praise.

Voice 2: For our ancestors who walked with Christ, for Peter, John, Andrew, Mary, Martha, and for those who kept the story alive and stayed faithful even in times of persecution — for Paul, Stephen, Lydia, and all the martyrs.

Congregation: God, we thank you for their strong faith.

Voice 3: For those whose names we remember who kept the faith alive through study, preaching, praying, writing down through the centuries, for Augustine, Aquinas, Martin Luther, John Calvin, John Knox, and many others too numerous to name.

Congregation: For all the saints, we give you thanks and praise.

Voice 4: For modern-day saints who never gave up no matter how bleak it looked, for Abraham Lincoln, Warren Wilson, Martin Luther King, Jr., Clara Barton, Mother Teresa — people who worked for the rights of people everywhere.

Congregation: We thank you for the Saints of God, faithful and loyal and true.

Leader: And we thank you for the Saints of this church, down through its history. *(Read a list of church leaders who have died)* Without them, *(Name of church)* would not have been able to give you honor and done your work in this place.

Congregation: For all the saints, who from their labors rest, we give you thanks and praise.

(Sing For All The Saints*)*

Scripture Readings
Matthew 5:1-12: *For this passage, have the congregation assist in the reading by placing one of the nine beatitudes in each bulletin. Make sure they are numbered 1 through 9 so that people will know the order. When it is time to read the passage, ask the congregation to find their particular beatitude in their bulletin. Explain that you will begin reading this scripture passage, but when you get to the part that says, "Then he began to speak, and taught them saying," you want them to read their beatitudes in numerical order. They might even read them as: "One: Blessed are the poor in spirit.... Two: Blessed are those who mourn...." So that they will stay in order. After the last beatitude is read, you will finish by reading verse 12.*

Revelation 7:9-17: *This passage is such a dramatic passage that it would be wonderful to have a storyteller tell it from memory. It's an unbelievable, yet exciting picture that is being painted, and could be best done by someone skilled in drama.*

Call to Offering
On behalf of all the saints who have gone before us, and for those who are yet to come, let us give God glory as we collect the morning offering.

Prayer of Dedication
Wonderful God, on this day of remembering the saints of our faith, may our gifts go to those who need it most: the hungry, the thirsty, the homeless, the war-torn, the grieving. Bless these gifts we bring to your glory. Amen.

Benediction (based on 1 John 3)
Leader: See what love our God has given us, that we should be called children of God; and that is what we are.
People: The reason the world does not know us is that it does not know God.
Leader: Beloved, we are God's children now; go and show the world the love of Christ.
People: We will spread the good news of God's love to those whom we meet.
Leader: May the peace of God which passes all understanding go with you. Amen.

Proper 26
Ordinary Time 31
Pentecost 24

Joshua 3:7-17   Psalm 107:1-7, 33-37
1 Thessalonians 2:9-13   Matthew 23:1-12

Hymns
Ask Me What Great Things I Know (NCH49, UM163, CBH337)
O Savior (Master), Let Me Walk With You (NCH503, UM430, CBH357, PH357)
Won't You Let Me Be Your Servant? (NCH539)
Now Thank We All Our God (PH555, NCH419, CBH85, 86, UM102)
God Is Here! (NCH70, PH461, UM660)
I Want Jesus To Walk With Me (NCH490, PH363, UM521, CBH439)
Today We Are All Called To Be (PH434)
Lord, Speak To Me (LBW403, NCH531, PH426, UM463, CBH499)

Anthems
Cry Unto The Lord, Ellen M. Keating, Mark Foster, SSA
Saints Bound For Heaven, Robert Shaw/Alice Parker, G. Schirmer
I Want Jesus To Walk With Me, arr. Hopson, CGA, 2-part/2-part mixed, trombone
Thank You, God, Austin Lovelace, CGA, Unison (good for young children)

Call to Worship (based on Psalm 107)
Leader: O give thanks to Yahweh whose steadfast love endures forever.
People: Let us thank Yahweh for his steadfast love, for all wonderful works to humankind.
Leader: Yahweh satisfies the thirsty, and fills the hungry with good things.
People: Yahweh turns rivers into a desert, springs of water into thirsty ground.
Leader: Yahweh turns a desert into pools of water, a parched land into springs of water.
People: And there the hungry live, and they establish a town to live in;
All: They sow fields, and plant vineyards, and get a fruitful yield. Praise Yahweh for great goodness.

Prayer of Invocation
Great and wondrous God, thank you for your goodness to your people throughout time. You continue to walk with us today, and we invoke your presence over this body as we give you thanks and glory. Infuse us with the Holy Spirit so that we can see what is real and holy in our world. Give us courage to follow you and do what you would have us do in our every day lives. God is here! And we your people meet to offer praise and prayer. Amen.

Scripture Readings
Joshua 3:7-17: *This passage is about another river crossing, but this one is going to somewhere instead of escaping from the Egyptians. It is an exciting story and one in which all the children through sixth grade could be involved. If you are a small congregation, you might invite the teens to join in this re-enactment for the congregation. In fact, depending on your focus in this*

service you might ask the whole congregation to "cross the Jordan" and come into the promised land as a sort of "commitment to faith." One could use the space between the pews and the chancel as the river. If the Sunday school children act this out, you will only need three speakers: the Voice of God, Joshua, and a Narrator. The participants will be divided into twelve groups, each one with its own leader. There will also be four Ark of the Covenant bearers, each holding one end of a rod on which the Ark is sitting. (Perhaps one of the classes can make the Ark of the Covenant as a project.) The Voice of God will be off-stage and not seen by the congregation. Joshua can be standing in the middle of the center aisle, and the participants can be at the back of the sanctuary divided into the twelve tribes of Israel. The Narrator can be at the lectern or pulpit.

Narrator: The Lord said to Joshua,

Voice of God: This day I will begin to exalt you in the sight of all Israel, so that they may know that I will be with you as I was with Moses. You are the one who shall command the priests who bear the Ark of the Covenant, "When you come to the edge of the waters of the Jordan, you shall stand still in the Jordan."

Joshua: *(Walking back toward the Israelites)* Draw near and hear the words of Yahweh. *(Israelites begin walking up the aisle toward Joshua. Stay in tribes)* "By this you shall know that among you is the living God who without fail will drive out from before you the Canaanites, Hittites, Hivites, Perizzites, Girgashites, Amorites, and Jebusites: The Ark of the Covenant of the Lord of all the earth is going to pass before you into the Jordan. So now select twelve men from the tribes of Israel, one from each tribe. When the soles of the feet of the priests who bear the ark of the Lord, the Lord of all the earth, rest in the waters of the Jordan, the waters of the Jordan flowing from above shall be off; they shall stand in a single heap." *(Points to the left, Israelites look to the left)*

Narrator: *(Four priests bring the ark to the front of all the other participants)* When the people set out from their tents to cross over the Jordan, the priests bearing the Ark of the Covenant were in front of the people. *(Everyone begins moving down the aisle toward the river)* Now the Jordan overflows all its banks throughout the time of harvest. So when those who bore the ark had come to the Jordan, and the feet of the priests bearing the ark were dipped in the edge of the water *(Priests walk into the space where the river is — stay there)*, the waters flowing from above stood still, rising up in a single heap far off at Adam, the city that is beside Zarethan, *(People point, look, gasp)*, while those flowing toward the sea of the Arabah, the Dead Sea, were wholly cut off. Then the people crossed over opposite Jericho. *(People begin walking across, gather up in the chancel area)* While all Israel were crossing over on dry ground, the priests who bore the Ark of the Covenant of the Lord stood on dry ground in the middle of the Jordan, until the entire nation finished crossing over the Jordan. *(If you decide to ask the congregation to cross over also, then end the reading as follows)*

Pastor: The Word of God for the People of God.

People: Thanks be to God.

Pastor: Let us remember the wonderful saving grace of Yahweh by recommitting ourselves to allow God to lead us where God wants us to go. If we are asked to cross a river on our own journeys of faith, let us trust God to lead us across.

People: We recommit ourselves this day to trust God to guide us. Today is a new beginning for each of us.

(Sing Today We Are All Called To Be *as Congregation returns to seats)*

Matthew 23:1-12: *This passage is a good follow-up because Jesus is reminding the people that God is their real leader, not other people. This passage can be read by one person, or it could be read by a choral speaking choir.*

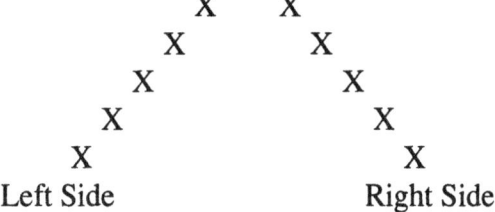

One Voice: Then Jesus said to the crowds and to his disciples,

Left Side: The scribes and the Pharisees sit on Moses' seat; therefore, do whatever they teach you and follow it:

Right Side: But do not do as they do, for they do not practice what they teach.

Left Side: They tie up heavy burdens, hard to bear, and lay them on the shoulders of others;

Right Side: But they themselves are unwilling to lift a finger to move them.

Left Side: They do all their deeds to be seen by others; for they make their phylacteries broad and their fringes long.

Right Side: They love to have the place of honor at banquets and the best seats in the synagogues,

Left Side: And to be greeted with respect in the marketplaces, and to have people call them rabbi.

Right Side: But you are not to be called rabbi, for you have one teacher, and you are all students.

All: And call no one your father on earth, for you have one Father — the one in heaven.

Left Side: Nor are you to be called instructors, for you have one instructor, the Messiah.

Right Side: The greatest among you will be your servant.

All: All who exalt themselves will be humbled, and all who humble themselves will be exalted.

Prayer of Dedication (after Offering)
O God, as we rededicate our lives to you by crossing over the dry riverbed, let us also rededicate ourselves to work for justice and peace in the world. May the gifts we bring be used toward that goal. May we work together toward the peaceful world that you envisioned when you created all of us. In Jesus' name. Amen.

Benediction
We have rededicated ourselves to do God's work in the world and to further our own relationship with our God. Stay strong and committed in furthering God's word. As Paul said to the Thessalonians, "When you received the Word of God heard today through human voices, accept it now not as a human word but as what it really is, God's word, which is also at work in all believers." Go in peace, love, and joy. Amen.

Proper 27
Ordinary Time 32
Pentecost 25

Joshua 24:1-3a, 14-25   Psalm 78:1-7
1 Thessalonians 4:13-18   Matthew 25:1-13

Hymns
Hark! The Herald Angels Sing (NCH144, CBH201, UM240, PH31, 32)
Once In Royal David's City (NCH145, UM250, PH49)
Steal Away (NCH599, CBH612, UM704)
Keep Your Lamps Trimmed And Burning (NCH369)
Lead On, O Cloud Of Presence/O King Eternal (CBH419, UM580, PH447, 448)
Sleepers, Wake! (CBH188, UM720, PH17, LBW31)
Rejoice! Rejoice, Believers (PH15, LBW25)
All People That On Earth Do Dwell (LBW245, NCH7, PH220, 221, UM75, CBH42)
O Lord, How Shall I Meet You? (LBW23, PH11)

Anthems
Give Me Oil In My Lamp, Max Exner, Carl Fischer
As For Me And My House, Morris Chapman, Maranatha! *Praise Book 4,* p. 152
Rejoice, Rejoice, Believers, Honore, CGA, 2-part mixed
Once In Royal David's City, arr. Pelz, CGA, Unison/2-part, congregtion, organ, C treble instrument

Call to Worship (based on Psalm 78)
Leader: Give ear, O my people, to my teaching; incline your ears to the words of my mouth. I will tell you many things that our ancestors have told us.
People: We will not hide them from the children; we will tell to the coming generation the glorious deeds and wonders of mighty God.
Leader: God established a decree in Jacob, and appointed a law in Israel, and commanded our ancestors to teach them to their children; that the next generation might know them, the children yet unborn, and rise up and tell them to their children,
People: So that they should set their hope in God, and not forget the works of God, but keep all commandments. Praise God!

Call to Confession
Joshua told his people, "Choose this day whom you will serve," and they chose to serve God. We also want to serve God, but we often fall short. Let us confess our shortcomings before our God.

Prayer of Confession
God of the ages, how often have your people fallen short of your expectations? We know the answer because we do it ourselves almost constantly. You ask so much of us, God — and there are so many distractions. We say we will meditate on your word, but there's such a good program on the television. We say we will spend Saturday working for the homeless, but we're not sure we can commit because someone might have a party. We try to come to church regularly,

but there's the kids' soccer game, and the Redskins *(or your team)* are playing at 1 o'clock. Forgive us, God. We know nothing is as important as spending time with you. Help us to get our priorities straight and to model them for our children — so that in turn they can know how to tell their own children. Faith lasts because it is passed from generation to generation. Help us to remember to keep the faith. Amen.

Assurance of Forgiveness
Leader: Jesus said, "Let the children come to me for such is the kingdom of God." Let the children tell us the good news.
Children: Jesus died for our sins. Isn't that great?
People: In Jesus Christ we are forgiven. Alleluia! Amen.

Scripture Readings
Joshua 24:1-3a, 14-25: *This passage can be read as a responsive reading between Joshua and the people. Joshua would move among the congregation as it is read, and his part be read with much drama. Joshua is very persistent in this passage. The words "Joshua said," and "the people said," can be omitted.*

Congregation: Then Joshua gathered all the tribes of Israel to Shechem, and summoned the elders, the heads, the judges, and the officers of Israel; and they presented themselves before God. And Joshua said to all the people,

Joshua: Thus says the Lord, the God of Israel: Long ago your ancestors — Terah and his sons Abraham and Nahor — lived beyond the Euphrates and served other gods. Then I took your father Abraham from beyond therRiver and led him through all the land of Canaan and made his offspring many. Now therefore revere the Lord, and serve him in sincerity and in faithfulness; put away the gods that your ancestors served beyond the river and in Egypt, and serve the Lord. Now if you are unwilling to serve the Lord, choose this day whom you will serve, whether the gods your ancestors served in the region beyond the river or the gods of the Amorites in whose land you are living; but as for me and my household, we will serve the Lord.

Congregation: Then the people answered, "Far be it from us that we should forsake the Lord to serve other gods; for it is the Lord our God who brought us and our ancestors up from the land of Egypt, out of the house of slavery, and who did those great signs in our sight. He protected us along all the way that we went, and among all the peoples through whom we passed; and the Lord drove out before us all the peoples, the Amorites who lived in the land. Therefore we also will serve the Lord, for he is our God." But Joshua said to the people,

Joshua: You cannot serve the Lord, for he is a holy God. He is a jealous God; he will not forgive your transgressions or your sins. If you forsake the Lord and serve foreign gods, then he will turn and do you harm, and consume you, after having done you good.

Congregation: And the people said to Joshua, "No, we will serve the Lord!" Then Joshua said to the people,

Joshua: You are witnesses against yourselves that you have chosen the Lord, to serve him.

Congregation: We are witnesses. He said,

Joshua: Then put away the foreign gods that are among you, and incline your hearts to the Lord, the God of Israel.

Congregation: The people said to Joshua, "The Lord our God we will serve, and him we will obey."

All: So Joshua made a covenant with the people that day, and made statutes and ordinances for them at Shechem.

Matthew 25:1-13: *This passage is really a good one for the choral speaking choir, using ten people as the bridesmaids and one person as the bridegroom. Have the bridesmaids come to the chancel in pairs, splitting off into two rows of five. The bridegroom will not enter until later in the passage. He will come slowly from the back of the congregation.*

```
         W     F
         W     F
         W      F
         W       F
         W        F
            BG
```

All: Then the kingdom of heaven will be like this. Ten bridesmaids took their lamps and went to meet the bridegroom.

Foolish: Five of them were foolish,

Wise: *(With a lower and wiser voice)* and five were wise.

Foolish: When the foolish took their lamps, they took no oil with them;

Wise: But the wise took flasks of oil with their lamps.

All: As the bridegroom was delayed, all of them became drowsy and slept. But at midnight there was a shout:

One Voice: Look! Here is the bridegroom! Come out to meet him. *(Bridegroom begins slowly coming down the aisle)*

All: Then all those bridesmaids got up and trimmed their lamps.

Foolish: The foolish said to the wise: "Give us some of your oil, for our lamps are going out."

Wise: But the wise replied, "No! there will not be enough for you and for us; you had better go to the dealers and buy some for yourselves." *(Foolish bridesmaids turn around away from the others)* And while they went to buy it, the bridegroom came *(Bridegroom stands on side of the Wise)*, and those who were ready went with him into the wedding banquet *(Bridegroom and Wise turn away)*, and the door was shut.

Foolish: *(Turn back toward Wise Bridesmaids)* Later the other bridesmaids came also, saying, "Lord, Lord, open to us."

Bridegroom: Truly I tell you, I do not know you. *(All turn back facing congregation)*

All: Keep awake therefore, for you know neither the day nor the hour.

Call to Offering
Let us waken to God's call to give freely of what we have. The ushers will wait upon us for the morning offering.

Prayer of Dedication
O God, how shall we meet you? Shall we come to you knowing that we have given what we could? Can we say, "As for me and my house, we will serve the Lord"? Please accept our gifts today to serve the world so that when you come again, the world will be ready to serve you with great gladness. Amen.

Benediction (based on Joshua 24)
Leader: It is God who brought us and our ancestors up from the land of Egypt, out of the house of slavery, and who did great signs in our sight.
People: He protected us along all the way that we went, and among all the peoples through whom we passed.
Leader: This same God continues to protect people who believe and serve.
People: As for us, we will choose the Lord, and we will obey.
Leader: In the name of the God who leads us, Christ who saves us, and the Holy Spirit who gives us energy for the journey. Amen.

Proper 28
Ordinary Time 33
Pentecost 26

Judges 4:1-7   Psalm 123
1 Thessalonians 5:1-11 Matthew 25:14-30

Hymns
Awake My Soul, Stretch Every Nerve (NCH491, CBH609)
Battle Hymn Of The Republic (NCH610, UM717)
O Day Of God, Draw Near (NCH611, CBH370, UM730, PH452)
God Of Grace And God Of Glory (NCH436, CBH366, UM577, PH420)
We Who Would Valiant Be (NCH494)
O God, Our Help In Ages Past (NCH25, CBH328, UM117)
When I Had Not Yet Learned Of Jesus/Yee Jun Ae Joo Nim Eul Nae Ka Mol La (PH410)
Come, Labor On (PH415, NCH532)
This Little Light Of Mine (CBH401, NCH524, 525, UM585)

Anthems
Thou That Dwellest In The Heavens, Malcolm Williamson, Boosey and Hawkes, Unison
O Savior Of The World, John Goss, G. Schirmer, SATB
Lord Jesus, Be My Song, Ken Kosche, CGA, Unison (good for young children)
A Mighty Fortress Is Our God, arr. Patterson, CGA, SAB, SATB, optional trumpet

Call to Worship
Leader: Arise, your light has come. It is now time to worship God.
People: Christ is the light of the world.
Leader: Don't hide your light under a bushel.
People: We let our light shine for all the world to see.
Leader: Now that the light shines forth in the world,
People: Let us take the warmth of that light and share it with those who are in darkness.
Leader: Let us come together to praise God.

Prayer of Thanksgiving
Gracious and loving God, as the days grow shorter, we are so grateful for the light of the sun, and for the warmth it gives to the earth. We thank you for the seasons of the year, and the changes they cause in us. They remind us that we are people of the earth, the earth that you created. We thank you, God, for the rhythms of the seasons, and especially for autumn. Autumn reminds us so much of our relationship with you, and our dependence on your grace. Thank you, God, for the season of harvest, as we gather in, and then make decisions on the distribution of our riches. Help us to be good stewards of your grace, both in what we give to others and in that which we keep for ourselves. Help us remember that it is more blessed to give than to receive — that and you have gifted us with so much. We are your grateful people. Amen.

Scripture Readings

1 Thessalonians 5:1-11: *This passage can either be read in the traditional way by one reader or can be done by a choral speaking choir.*

```
4 5 6   10 11 12
1 2 3    7  8  9
```

Voices 1-6: Now concerning the times and the seasons, brothers and sisters, you do not need to have anything written to you.

Voices 7-12: For you yourselves know very well that the day of the Lord will come like a thief in the night.

Voice 1: When they say,

Voice 9: There is peace and security,

Voice 1: Then sudden destruction will come upon them as labor pains come upon a pregnant woman,

Voices 4-6: And there will be no escape!

Voices 7-12: But you, beloved, are not in darkness, for that day to surprise you like a thief;

All: For you are all children of light and children of the day; we are not of the night or of darkness. So then let us not fall asleep as others do, but let us keep awake and be sober;

Voices 2-3: For those who sleep sleep at night,

Voices 7-8: And those who are drunk get drunk at night.

All: But since we belong to the day, let us be sober, and put on the breastplate of faith and love, and for a helmet the hope of salvation.

Voices 1-6: For God has destined us not for wrath but for obtaining salvation through our Lord Jesus Christ,

Voices 7-12: Who died for us, so that whether we are awake or asleep we may live with them.

All: Therefore encourage one another and build up each other, as indeed you are doing.

Matthew 25:14-30: *This passage is the familiar parable of the talents. It would be a good parable to recreate dramatically, but the ending is harsh; so have older students recreate it. Perhaps the senior high class could work with this passage and give it a modern edge. It could take place on Wall Street, and could include a group of traders working with a wealthy, but cruel client. If you want it to be read as written, then it still could be done dramatically. Cast would include a Narrator, Wealthy Landowner, 5-talent Slave, 2-talent Slave, and 1-talent Slave for a cast of five.*

Call to Offering

During this Stewardship season as we ponder how to distribute the gifts God has given us, let us bring some of those gifts to God as we collect the morning offering.

Prayer of Dedication

Glorious God, we bring you what we have, however we may decide. Now help us use it in your service and to your glory; remembering how Jesus gave of himself for us. Amen.

Benediction

Leader: To you, O God, we lift our eyes, marveling at your goodness.
People: Help us be good to those we meet, sharing more of ourselves than we think is necessary.
Leader: Use your gifts and they will multiply; hide them and they will gather moss.
People: We will use the many gifts God has bestowed upon us.
Leader: Use them for good, in the name of God who created us, Christ who loves us, and the Holy Spirit who gives us aid. Amen.

Christ The King
Proper 29

Ezekiel 34:11-16, 20-24   Psalm 100
Ephesians 1:15-23   Matthew 25:31-46

Hymns
Savior, Like A Shepherd Lead Us (CBH355, NCH252, UM381, PH387, LBW481)
Open Now Thy Gates Of Beauty (CBH19, PH489)
All People That On Earth Do Dwell (CBH42, NCH7, UM75, PH220, 221)
Rejoice, The Lord Is King! (CBH288, NCH303alt., UM715, 716, PH155, LBW171)
Will (Won't) You Let Me Be Your Servant? (CBH307, NCH539)
Lord, Whose Love In Humble Service (CBH369, UM581, PH427)
We Give Thee But Thine Own (CBH384, PH428)
The Church Of Christ In Every Age (CBH403, NCH306, UM589, PH421)
A Hymn Of Glory Let Us Sing (NCH259, PH141)
Cuando El Pobre/When The Poor Ones (UM434, PH407)
Now Thank We All Our God (PH555, UM102, NCH419, CBH85, 86)
Crown Him With Many Crowns (PH151, UM327, NCH301, CBH116, LBW170)

Anthems
Praise God From Whom All Blessings Flow, William P. Rowan, GIA, SATB
Psalm 100, Hal Hopson, Hope, Unison/SA/optional SATB, brass, woodwinds, strings, Orff
Savior, Like A Shepherd Lead Us, Hal Hopson, CGA, 2-part
Shout For Joy, Kerrick, CGA, 2-part

Call to Worship (based on Psalm 100)
Leader: Make a joyful noise to the Lord, all the earth.
Men: Worship God with gladness; come into God's presence with singing.
Women: Know that the Lord is God. God made us, and we are God's people, and the sheep of God's pasture.
Leader: Enter God's gates with thanksgiving and into the courts with praise. Give thanks and bless God's name.
All: For the Lord is good; God's steadfast love endures forever, and God's faithfulness to all generations.

Prayer of Confession
God, we confess to you our shortcomings and our fears. We don't know how to be faithful to you. We are so busy with our own lives that we don't notice the person in our office who needs to have someone listen to him. We don't even know when we cut someone off in our cars or cause an accident because of our self-absorption. We are so tired we can't even stay awake to hear your word in this place. Help us, God. Open our eyes and our hearts to the sorrows and joys of your world. Slow us down so that we might share in this great world by helping others. We don't want to ask, "Lord, when was it that we saw you hungry and fed you?" Forgive us for our shortsightedness. Amen.

Assurance of Forgiveness
God has given Jesus Christ the power to guide us in wisdom and forgive us our shortcomings when God raised him from the dead and seated him at his right hand in heaven. This is the good news! In Jesus Christ we are forgiven.

Scripture Readings
Ephesians 1:15-23: *This passage is part of a letter (epistle) sent to the church in Ephesus. This passage can be read by one person with this introduction: "Brothers and sisters in Christ, recently I have received this wonderful letter from our beloved brother, Paul. He asks that I read it to you. Today I would like to share a portion of this important letter so that you may gain strength in your faith. I begin." Then read the letter with passion and hope. The beauty and passion of the words make it a perfect reading with which to use sign language or to be interpreted through modern dance.*

Matthew 25:31-46: *This passage would be enhanced dramatically by having people in the congregation recite some of the verses. Use a single reader for the most part, but have six members of your congregation (pre-chosen and rehearsed) stand one at a time, and read verses 35-36. They will sit on the **right** side of the congregation. Also choose three voices to sit on the **left** side of the congregation to read verses 37b-39. These voices will stand when it is their turn and sound as if they are challenging what is being said.*

Liturgist: And when the Son of Man comes in his glory, and all the angels with him, then he will sit on the throne of his glory. All the nations will be gathered before him, and he will separate people from one another as a shepherd separates the sheep from the goats, and he will put the sheep at his right hand and the goats at his left. Then the king will say to those at his right hand, "Come, you that are blessed by my Father, inherit the kingdom prepared for you from the foundation of the world."

Voice 1: For I was hungry and you gave me food,

Voice 2: I was thirsty and you gave me something to drink,

Voice 3: I was a stranger and you welcomed me.

Voice 4: I was naked and you gave me clothing

Voice 5: I was sick and you took care of me,

Voice 6: I was in prison and you visited me.

Liturgist: Then the righteous will answer him

Voice 7: Lord, when was it that we saw you hungry and gave you food, or thirsty and gave you something to drink?

Voice 8: And when was it that we saw you a stranger and welcomed you, or naked and gave you clothing?

Voice 9: And when was it that we saw you sick or in prison and visited you?

Liturgist: And the king will answer them, "Truly I tell you, just as you did it to one of the least of these who are members of my family, you did it to me." Then he will say to those at his left hand, "You that are accursed, depart from me into the eternal fire prepared for the devil and his angels; for I was hungry and you gave me no food, I was thirsty and you gave me nothing to drink, I was a stranger and you did not welcome me, naked and you did not give me clothing, sick and in prison and you did not visit me." Then they also will answer,

Voices 7, 8, and 9: Lord, when was it that we saw you hungry or thirsty or a stranger or naked or sick or in prison, and did not take care of you? *(Voices strong, but a little frightened)*

Liturgist: Then he will answer them, "Truly I tell you, just as you did not do it to one of the least of these, you did not do it to me. And these will go away into eternal punishment, but the righteous into eternal life."

Call to Offering
God wants all of us to inherit the kingdom prepared for us by the foundation of the world. As the ushers wait upon us for our offering, let us give freely to build up the kingdom.

Prayer of Dedication
Leader: May the gifts we have received be used to help the hungry and thirsty, the stranger and the one in need of clothing and shelter, the sick and the prisoner.
People: Jesus said, "Just as you do these things for the least of these who are members of my family, you did it to me." Amen.

Benediction
Leader: With your eyes and your heart enlightened, may you know the hope to which Christ has called you, and the riches of his glorious inheritance among the saints.
People: Open the eyes of our heart so that we may feel the joy and pain of the world. In this way we let Christ into our hearts. Amen.

Thanksgiving Day

Deuteronomy 8:7-18 **Psalm 65**
2 Corinthians 9:6-15 **Luke 17:11-19**

Hymns
We Plow The Fields And Scatter (CBH96, PH560)
Sing To The Lord Of Harvest (CBH98)
Creating God, Your Fingers Trace (CBH168, NCH462, UM109, PH134)
For The Fruit Of All Creation (CBH90, NCH425, UM97, PH553)
God, Whose Giving Knows No Ending (CBH383 NCH565, PH422)
The Church Of Christ In Every Age (CBH403, NCH306, UM589, PH421)
Amazing Grace, How Sweet The Sound (PH280, UM378, NCH547-548, CBH143)
Come, Ye Thankful People, Come (PH551, UM694, NCH422, CBH94, LBW407)
Let All Things Now Living (PH554)

Anthems
Sing To The Lord Of The Harvest, Healey Willan, Concordia, SATB
O Sing The Glories Of The Lord, H. K. Andrews, Oxford, SATB
Sing Thankful Songs/Cantad cancion de gratitude, arr. Gay, CGA, Unison/2-part, optional flute, handbells
Let All Things Now Living, arr. Cherwien, CGA, Unison/2-part, congregation, optional flute

Often Thanksgiving Day services are shared services between congregations. If you haven't done this, you might invite some nearby churches to worship together either on Thanksgiving Eve or Thanksgiving morning. The different choirs could offer anthems. The scripture passages lend themselves well to a modified service of scripture and hymns. The scripture passages speak well for themselves; therefore a sermon may not be necessary. If you decide not to have a sermon, an extended time of prayer might be appropriate. You might have slips of paper cut into pumpkin (or some other shape showing God's bounty) shapes in each bulletin. There could be a time of silence in which people could write their own prayers of thanksgiving and then either put them in an offering plate or on a bulletin board as they leave.

Call to Worship (based on Psalm 65)
Leader: Praise is due to you, O God, in Zion; and to you shall vows be performed.
People: Happy are those whom you choose and bring near to live in your courts. We shall be satisfied with the goodness of your house, your holy temple.
Leader: By awesome deeds you answer us with deliverance, O God of our salvation; you are the hope of all the ends of the earth and of the farthest seas.
People: By your strength you established the mountains; you are girded with might.
Leader: You silence the roaring of the seas, the roaring of their waves, the tumult of the peoples.
People: Those who live at earth's farthest bounds are awed by your signs;
All: You make the gateways of the morning and the evening shout for joy.

Opening Hymn
Let All Things Now Living

Prayer of Adoration
Bountiful God, we gather for a service of thanksgiving to give honor for all you have given us. We live in a world that you have created for us, and we are grateful. We have so much and it is because of you. You are a great and awesome God, filled with compassion and love for your created order. Thank you for your steadfastness even as we continue to fall short of your expectations. Give us fortitude, God, so that we may know what you would have us do and the courage to do it always. Amen.

Service of Scripture and Hymns (Deuteronomy 8:7-18 and the hymn *God Whose Giving Knows No Ending*)
Liturgist: For the Lord your God is bringing you into a good land, a land with flowing streams, with springs and underground waters welling up in valleys and hills, a land of wheat and barley, of vines and fig trees and pomegranates, a land of olive trees and honey, a land where you may eat bread without scarcity, where you will lack nothing, a land whose stones are iron and from whose hills you may mine copper. You shall eat your fill and bless the Lord your God for the good land that he has given you.

(Congregation sings verse 1 of the hymn)

Liturgist: Take care that you do not forget the Lord your God, by failing to keep his commandments, his ordinances, and his statutes, which I am commanding you today. When you have eaten your fill and have built fine houses and live in them, and when your herds and flocks have multiplied, and your silver and gold is multiplied, and all that you have is multiplied, then do not exalt yourself, forgetting the Lord your God, who brought you out of the land of Egypt, out of the house of slavery, who led you through the great and terrible wilderness, an arid wasteland with poisonous snakes and scorpions. He made water flow for you from flint rock, and fed you in the wilderness with manna that your ancestors did not know, to humble you and to test you, and in the end to do you good.

(Choir sings verse 2 of the hymn)

Liturgist: Do not say to yourself, "My power and the might of my own hand have gotten me this wealth." But remember the Lord your God, for it is he who gives you power to get wealth, so that he may confirm his covenant that he swore to your ancestors, as he is doing today.

(Congregation and choir sing verse 3 together)

2 Corinthians 9:6-15: *This passage would be well done by a storyteller. If none of the congregations has one, perhaps one could be hired for this service. They could also read the Deuteronomy passage, if needed.*

Hymn
We Plow The Fields And Scatter

Luke 17:11-19: *Use a choral speaking choir.*

```
                                    L  L L L
                Jesus               HL L L
    Narrator                        L  L L
```

Narrator: On the way to Jerusalem Jesus was going through the region between Samaria and Galilee. As he entered a village, ten lepers approached him. Keeping their distance, they called out, saying,

Lepers: Jesus, Jesus, Master, Master *(Coming at different times from different people — then say together)*, have mercy on us!

Narrator: When he saw them, he said to them,

Jesus: Go and show yourselves to the priests. *(Lepers turn facing away from Jesus)*

Narrator: And as they went, they were made clean. Then one of them, when he saw that he was healed, turned back *(Healed Leper turns back toward Jesus)*, praising God with a loud voice.

Healed Leper: Praise God, praise God! I'm healed. Thank you, Jesus.

Narrator: He prostrated himself at Jesus' feet and thanked him, and he was a Samaritan. Then Jesus asked,

Jesus: Were not ten made clean? But the other nine, where are they? Was none of them found to return and give praise to God except this foreigner? Get up and go on your way; your faith has made you well.

Hymn
Amazing Grace

Time of Prayer
    Bidding Prayers offered by the Pastor and Congregation
    Silence for writing personal prayers
    Prayers collected as offering
    The Doxology

Closing Hymn
For The Fruit Of All Creation

Benediction (based on Deuteronomy 8)
Leader: Take care that you do not forget your God by failing to keep the commandments and statutes.
People: When we return to our fine houses and have eaten our fill, and when all we have has been multiplied, we will remember our God and all God's goodness.
Leader: It is God who gives you the ability to gather in your bounty. Confirm the covenant God gave to your ancestors, as God continues to covenant with us today.
People: Praise to the God of harvest. May we share what we have with those who need it.
Leader: Go in the name of the God who loves all of us. Amen.

U.S. / Canadian Lectionary Comparison

The following index shows the correlation between the Sundays and special days of the church year as they are titled or labeled in the Revised Common Lectionary published by the Consultation On Common Texts and used in the United States (the reference used for this book) and the Sundays and special days of the church year as they are titled or labeled in the Revised Common Lectionary used in Canada.

Revised Common Lectionary	**Canadian Revised Common Lectionary**
Advent 1	Advent 1
Advent 2	Advent 2
Advent 3	Advent 3
Advent 4	Advent 4
Christmas Eve	Christmas Eve
Nativity Of The Lord / Christmas Day	The Nativity Of Our Lord
Christmas 1	Christmas 1
January 1 / Holy Name of Jesus	January 1 / The Name Of Jesus
Christmas 2	Christmas 2
Epiphany Of The Lord	The Epiphany Of Our Lord
Baptism Of The Lord / Epiphany 1	The Baptism Of Our Lord / Proper 1
Epiphany 2 / Ordinary Time 2	Epiphany 2 / Proper 2
Epiphany 3 / Ordinary Time 3	Epiphany 3 / Proper 3
Epiphany 4 / Ordinary Time 4	Epiphany 4 / Proper 4
Epiphany 5 / Ordinary Time 5	Epiphany 5 / Proper 5
Epiphany 6 / Ordinary Time 6	Epiphany 6 / Proper 6
Epiphany 7 / Ordinary Time 7	Epiphany 7 / Proper 7
Epiphany 8 / Ordinary Time 8	Epiphany 8 / Proper 8
Transfiguration Of The Lord / Last Sunday After Epiphany	The Transfiguration Of Our Lord / Last Sunday After Epiphany
Ash Wednesday	Ash Wednesday
Lent 1	Lent 1
Lent 2	Lent 2
Lent 3	Lent 3
Lent 4	Lent 4
Lent 5	Lent 5
Passion / Palm Sunday (Lent 6)	Passion / Palm Sunday
Holy / Maundy Thursday	Holy / Maundy Thursday
Good Friday	Good Friday
Resurrection Of The Lord / Easter	The Resurrection Of Our Lord
Easter 2	Easter 2
Easter 3	Easter 3
Easter 4	Easter 4
Easter 5	Easter 5
Easter 6	Easter 6
Ascension Of The Lord	The Ascension Of Our Lord
Easter 7	Easter 7
Day Of Pentecost	The Day Of Pentecost
Trinity Sunday	The Holy Trinity
Proper 4 / Pentecost 2 / O T 9*	Proper 9
Proper 5 / Pent 3 / O T 10	Proper 10
Proper 6 / Pent 4 / O T 11	Proper 11
Proper 7 / Pent 5 / O T 12	Proper 12
Proper 8 / Pent 6 / O T 13	Proper 13
Proper 9 / Pent 7 / O T 14	Proper 14

Proper 10 / Pent 8 / O T 15	Proper 15
Proper 11 / Pent 9 / O T 16	Proper 16
Proper 12 / Pent 10 / O T 17	Proper 17
Proper 13 / Pent 11 / O T 18	Proper 18
Proper 14 / Pent 12 / O T 19	Proper 19
Proper 15 / Pent 13 / O T 20	Proper 20
Proper 16 / Pent 14 / O T 21	Proper 21
Proper 17 / Pent 15 / O T 22	Proper 22
Proper 18 / Pent 16 / O T 23	Proper 23
Proper 19 / Pent 17 / O T 24	Proper 24
Proper 20 / Pent 18 / O T 25	Proper 25
Proper 21 / Pent 19 / O T 26	Proper 26
Proper 22 / Pent 20 / O T 27	Proper 27
Proper 23 / Pent 21 / O T 28	Proper 28
Proper 24 / Pent 22 / O T 29	Proper 29
Proper 25 / Pent 23 / O T 30	Proper 30
Proper 26 / Pent 24 / O T 31	Proper 31
Proper 27 / Pent 25 / O T 32	Proper 32
Proper 28 / Pent 26 / O T 33	Proper 33
Christ The King (Proper 29 / O T 34)	Proper 34 / Christ The King / Reign Of Christ
Reformation Day (October 31)	Reformation Day (October 31)
All Saints' Day (November 1 or 1st Sunday in November)	All Saints' Day (November 1)
Thanksgiving Day (4th Thursday of November)	Thanksgiving Day (2nd Monday of October)

*O T = Ordinary Time

www.ingramcontent.com/pod-product-compliance
Lightning Source LLC
Chambersburg PA
CBHW081216230426
43666CB00015B/2753